HOME AT LAST

PAM & STAN CAMPBELL

HOME AT LAST

VICTOR BOOKS®

A DIVISION OF SCRIPTURE PRESS PUBLICATIONS INC.
USA CANADA ENGLAND

BibleLog Thru the New Testament Series
Book 1 **When God Left Footprints** (Matthew thru John)
Book 2 **Good News to Go** (Acts thru 1 Corinthians)
Book 3 **Priority Mail** (2 Corinthians thru Philemon)
Book 4 **Home At Last** (Hebrews thru Revelation)

BibleLog Thru the Old Testament Series
Book 1 **Let There Be Life** (Genesis thru Ruth)
Book 2 **Who's Running This Kingdom?** (1 Samuel thru 2 Chronicles)
Book 3 **Tales, Tunes, and Truths** (Ezra thru Song of Songs)
Book 4 **Watchmen Who Wouldn't Quit** (Isaiah thru Malachi)

BibleLog for Adults is an inductive Bible study series designed to take you through the Bible in 2 years if you study one session each week. This eight-book series correlates with SonPower's **BibleLog** series for youth. You may want to use **BibleLog** in your daily quiet time, completing a chapter a week by working through a few pages each day. Or you may want to use this series (along with the SonPower **BibleLog** series) in family devotions with your teenagers. This book also includes a leader's guide for use in small groups.

Scripture taken from the *Holy Bible, New International Version,* © 1973, 1978, 1984, International Bible Society. Used by permission of Zondervan Bible Publishers.

Library of Congress Catalog Card Number: 91-65459
ISBN: 0-89693-870-0

Recommended Dewey Decimal Classification: 225
Suggested Subject Heading: BIBLE STUDY: NEW TESTAMENT

C O N T E N T S

24648

BEFORE YOU BEGIN

Welcome to Book 4 in the
BibleLog Thru the New Testament Series

Though the Bible continues to be one of the world's best-selling books, few people are familiar enough with it to comprehend "the big picture." They may know many of the specific stories about Abraham, Samson, Jonah, Jesus, Peter, Paul, and so forth. Yet most people are unsure how these characters fit into the broad historic groupings—patriarchs, judges, kings, prophets, Gospels, epistles, etc.

That's why we are introducing the **BibleLog Thru the New Testament Series.** The purpose of the **BibleLog** studies is to guide you through the New Testament in one year, at the rate of one session per week. This series eliminates the perceived drudgery of Bible reading by removing unnecessary references and explaining the material in clear terms that anyone can understand. The pace should be fast enough to propel you through the material without getting bogged down, yet slow enough to allow you to see things you never noticed before. First-time readers will feel completely at ease as they explore the Bible on their own. Yet no matter how many times a person has been through the Bible, this study will provide fresh insight.

WHAT MAKES BIBLELOG DIFFERENT?

Countless thousands of adults have, at some point in their lives, decided to read through the Bible. Pastors, Sunday School teachers, Bible study leaders, or peers have preached the benefits of "Read your Bible," "Get into the Word," "Meditate on Scripture," and so forth. And after hearing so many worthwhile challenges, a lot of determined, committed adults have dusted off the covers of their Bibles and set themselves to the task ahead.

They usually make a noble effort too. The first couple of Bible books whiz past before they know it. The next few books aren't quite as fast-paced, but they have their strong points. Then comes a tough passage. In most cases, the Gospels are enough to do in even the most eager readers. And instead of feeling like they've accomplished something, all that those people feel is guilt because they didn't finish what they started.

That's why this Bible study series was developed. It calls for a one-year commitment on your part to get through the New Testament. By following the session plans provided, you only need to complete one session each week to accomplish your one-year goal. You won't read the entire New Testament word-for-word, but you will go much more in-depth than most of the New Testament overviews you may have tried. You will still be challenged just to get through the major flow of New Testament action in one year.

WHAT ARE THE FEATURES OF BIBLELOG?

❑ **THE WHOLE BIBLE** Not a verse-by-verse study, but an approach that hits all the books without skipping major passages.

❑ **THE RIGHT PACE** By completing one session each week (a couple of pages per day), you will get through the New Testament in one year.

❑ **A FRESH APPROACH** The inductive design allows you to personally interact with biblical truth. Longer, drier passages are summarized in the text, and difficult passages are explained, but you are kept involved in the discovery process at all times.

❑ **INSTANT APPLICATION** Each weekly session concludes with a **Journey Inward** section of practical application that allows you to respond to the content immediately. The goal is to help you apply the truths of the Bible today.

❑ **GROUP STUDY OPTION** A leader's guide is included to promote discussion and further application, if desired. After a week of self-study, a time of group interaction can be very effective in reinforcing God's truth. Each book covers 13 weeks.

❑ **REASONABLE PRICE** The entire set of 4 New Testament BibleLog books costs no more than a basic Bible commentary. And after completing the series, you will have a self-written commentary of the New Testament for future reference.

❑ **48 DIFFERENT TOPICS** Over a one-year period of study, you will be challenged to apply what the Bible has to say about 48 different topics, including your relationship with Jesus, rejection, integrity, commitment, self-image, empathy, eternity, and much more.

HOW CAN YOU GET THE MOST OUT OF BIBLELOG?

We recommend a group study for this series, if possible. If group members work through the content of the sessions individually during the week, the time your group needs to spend going over facts will be greatly reduced. With the content portion completed prior to the group meeting, your group time can emphasize the application of the biblical concepts to your individual members. A leader's guide is included at the back of the book to direct you in a review of the content. But the real strength of the leader's guide is to show you how to apply what you are learning. If you don't have the opportunity to go through this series with a group, that's OK too. Just be sure to think through all the **Journey Inward** sections at the end of each session.

FROM THE AUTHORS

You might say that this book marks the beginning of the end. If you've been faithfully journeying through this **BibleLog** series, congratulations—you've made it to Book 4.

In this final book of the **BibleLog** Series, you will receive a good overview of your faith—from a perspective of past, present, and future. The Book of Hebrews will start you off with a look at the past—at the origins of many current worship practices as well as several Old Testament symbols that pointed to the coming of Jesus. The biblical books that follow will provide a lot of practical help for dealing with the issues you face every day—issues such as the desire for status, your speech habits, establishing role models, and so forth. The big finish is the Book of Revelation, which will give you a good understanding of what you can look forward to in the future. There you should discover why this book is titled *Home At Last.*

Keep one thing in mind as you go through these sessions: Whenever this book refers to the "author" or "writer" of a biblical book, it is a reference to the human being used by God to communicate His divine message. Paul's statement to Timothy still holds true: "All Scripture is God-breathed and is useful for teaching, rebuking, correcting and training in righteousness" (2 Timothy 3:16). Yet God has chosen to use a number of people with unique personalities and illustrations to record what we know as the Bible. Those people are important because they reinforce God's message with their own observations and eyewitness accounts.

May God provide the wisdom you need as you work your way through this book. And when you finish, may your knowledge of Him be stronger than it has ever been before.

Pam & Stan Campbell

The struggle for status never seems to end.

1

WHO'S NUMBER ONE?
(Hebrews 1:1–4:13)

The year was ending and, as Political Editor for the *Jonesboro Sentinel*, Rhonda must write an editorial reflecting on the events of the past year.

In retrospect, Rhonda could hardly believe that the city of Jonesboro had elected Jack Swanson as mayor. Jack was a nice enough guy, but he had absolutely no aptitude for leadership. What he did have was blond, wavy hair and perfect teeth. (And none of the other candidates for mayor had a chance after Jack's campaign posters were displayed and his TV ads went on the air.)

Larry Mulhoney, one of Jack's opponents, lost the election but wound up achieving many of the goals that should have been accomplished by Jack. Larry was a likable politician with a good sense of humor, but he was never quite admired like Jack. Rhonda (and many others) knew that Larry would have been the best choice for mayor, but the vote had been an overwhelming majority in Jack's favor.

As Rhonda gathered her thoughts for her editorial, she wondered about the motives of many of Jonesboro's political figures. *Why did Jack Swanson want to be mayor when he didn't want to do any of the work? Why did large groups of politicians and lawyers show up at rallies to be photographed with certain minority groups when they never went to any of the meetings otherwise? Why did the public elect people for high-level positions when all those people obviously cared about was themselves? Just how much would people be willing to sacrifice for just a little more status?*

Rhonda had seen people sacrifice time, money, reputation, health, other people's feelings, and much more to be "just a little more" popular with their contingency. In fact, some of the same people would probably put everything on the line again and again, spending millions of dollars, running for office so they could earn $200,000 a year.

 JOURNEY ONWARD

The struggle for status probably begins during your high school and college years. Oh, sure, later in life you contend for jobs, titles, promotions, raises, spouses, and such. But in high school, many of your peers mistakenly tried to make you think that your status was directly related to your worth as a person.

The church tries to address this issue by emphasizing the fact that Jesus "did not consider equality with God something to be grasped, but made Himself nothing, taking the very nature of a servant" (Philippians 2:6-7). This fact is true, of course. Yet sometimes we pay so much attention to the "nature of a servant" part that we neglect to place proper emphasis on the "equality with God" truth.

This session takes us into the Book of Hebrews, a book that leaves no question as to the godly status of Jesus Christ. Hebrews was first addressed to a number of Jewish (Hebrew) Christians who were very likely being urged to revert to Judaism or compromise their Christian faith with Jewish tradition. The writer of Hebrews makes it clear that Jesus was not your everyday ordinary rabbi. He is, indeed, the Messiah. He is God and is worthy of praise and worship. He is the fulfillment of everything God had promised the Jewish people in the Old Testament. As you go through the Book of Hebrews, look for all the comparisons the writer makes to capture the attention of people familiar with the Old Testament—Moses, the high priests, the tabernacle, Melchizedek, blood sacrifices, and so forth.

Hebrews is such a classic book of the Bible that the author certainly deserves some recognition. But since he or she is never identified in the book, Bible scholars to this day are unable to come to an agreement about who the writer was. Some think Hebrews is another of Paul's books, but it has a different style than most of Paul's other works (and Paul identified himself in his other letters). Other nominations for Name-that-Author have included Barnabas, Apollos, Luke, Philip, and Priscilla. While it would be nice to know who had penned this book, that fact is insignificant compared to what we can learn from the person's tremendous insight into the nature of Jesus. It should soon become clear that Hebrews was inspired by God just as all the other books with known authors.

Read Hebrews 1:1-3.
From the first verse, the writer makes it clear that he (or she) is going to be making some significant contrasts. When God had a message for people during the Old Testament era, how did He transmit that message? (Hebrews 1:1)

But these days, said the author, God has a much better way of communicating with us. Our knowledge of God increased a great deal when God sent Jesus into the world. So the writer of Hebrews immediately listed a number of significant facts about Jesus. Reread verses 2-3 and list everything you can find out about Jesus.

Now review the list you just made. Since these things are true about Jesus, what are some things you can deduce about God?

Better than Angels

As you can see, the writer didn't take long to express the fact that Jesus was no ordinary religious teacher. Clearly, no other human being could approach Jesus' level of importance. But how about nonhumans? How would Jesus compare with other supernatural beings? It seems that many of the Jewish people had a reverence for the angels of God because of the roles they played in the Old Testament. So the author of Hebrews contrasted Jesus to the angels.

Read Hebrews 1:4-14.
To begin with, the writer referred to the title of Jesus as the Son of God. Knowing that angels were occasionally referred to in the Old Testament as the "sons of God," how did he demonstrate that Jesus was even more special to God? (1:4-5)

What was a second argument the writer used to show that Jesus was superior to the angels? (1:6)

What was a third contrast between Jesus and the angels? (1:7-9)

But the writer isn't finished yet. What is still another way that Jesus is superior to angels? (1:10-14)

Getting Personal — *How does this description of angels compare with your previous thoughts about angels?*

Some of these verses may not have been exactly clear to you. But if you knew the Scripture as well as some of the Jewish people of that time did, you might have recognized no fewer than *seven* direct quotations from the Old Testament about Jesus (detailing His exalted position in relation to the angels and His equality with God the Father). Since the Book of Hebrews was directed to Jewish people, they were probably quick to make the connection between the Old Testament prophecies concerning the Messiah and what they knew to be true about Jesus' life, death, and resurrection. And while you may not be quite as quick to understand all the subtleties of these passages, you should still have come up with the obvious fact that Jesus has an exalted position of authority while the role of the angels is to serve and minister.

Read Hebrews 2:1-18.

It wasn't the intention of the writer to put down God's angels. Clearly, Jesus is superior to the angels, but the work of God's angels should still be very important to us. In fact, one of the reasons the Jews held the angels in such high regard was because they had been involved in God's giving the Law to Moses (Deuteronomy 33:2). Yet the angels' contributions cannot compare to what Jesus has done for us. So the author of Hebrews gave this argument: Since the Law (given by God with the assistance of His angels) is held in such high regard, and since Jesus is clearly superior to the angels, then think how important it is for us to acknowledge the salvation that Jesus provides for us! In what ways can we be sure that this salvation is authentic? (Hebrews 2:1-4)

One of the things that probably confused some of the Jewish people was that Jesus hadn't looked very important. Every time an angel is mentioned in the Bible, the person to whom he appears responds with fear and trembling. But Jesus hadn't had that effect on the people who knew Him. Again, the writer of Hebrews pulled out an Old Testament quotation (Psalm 8:4-6) to explain why Jesus may not have made as spectacular an impression as some of the angels. The passage was originally applied to humankind as a whole, but made even more sense when applied to Jesus. Why hadn't the coming of Jesus dazzled people as much as the appearance of an angel might have? (Hebrews 2:5-8)

What was the purpose of Jesus being "made a little lower than the angels"? (2:9)

Do you see what has happened here? Jesus, who is in every way God, willingly gave up His heavenly status to come to earth and live as a human. He who had been head of all Creation temporarily became lower than the angels whom He had helped create. But as soon as He died for humankind, He was "crowned with glory and honor," even though the world has yet to see Him back in His heavenly role as King of kings. Jesus' humanity — the conscious "lowering" of Himself — is the very thing that entitles Him to our praise and worship. How did Jesus' humanity alter our relationship with God? (2:10-15)

How did Jesus' humanity make Him better equipped to understand what we go through? (2:16-18)

In the next session you will see more about what it means to have Jesus as our "merciful and faithful High Priest." For now, it is enough to realize that because Jesus came to earth and went through all the hassles we go through, He can in every way relate to our feelings.

Much of the first part of the Book of Hebrews may have been addressing a belief by some of the Jewish people that angels would rule in Jesus' heavenly kingdom. The writer wanted to assure them that Jesus had made it possible for "mere" human beings to share in His glory and honor as "brothers."

The Not-So-Good Ol' Days
Read Hebrews 3:1-19.
Besides the angels, the Jewish people had another major hero — Moses. And since Moses held so much respect in the minds of the people, the writer of Hebrews also provided a contrast between Jesus and Moses. In what ways did he suggest that Jesus was superior to Moses? (3:1-6)

In a reference to Psalm 95:7-11, the author of Hebrews reminded his readers that the Jewish people under Moses had rebelled and disobeyed (Hebrews 3:7-11). And again the Jews were in danger of rebellion — this time against Jesus (who was greater than Moses). What advice did the author give them to help them avoid falling into sin? (3:12-13)

Getting Personal — *What role(s) do your Christian friends play in helping you be true to God?*

The writer then reminded the people that Moses had problems with the very people who had been rescued from the slavery of Egypt. Consequently, those people weren't allowed to enter the Promised Land. As a parallel, some of the Jewish people were considering giving up on their belief in Jesus. What did the writer of Hebrews remind them to do if they really wanted to "share in Christ"? (3:14-19)

Read Hebrews 4:1-13.
For those people who were wavering in their decision to follow Jesus, what kind of hope did the writer of Hebrews provide? (4:1)

Continuing his comparison to the Old Testament people of Israel, the writer pointed out that the Promised Land was a "rest" for the Israelites who had come out of slavery and wandered in the desert. This temporary rest in the Promised Land symbolizes the eternal rest we can eventually have with God in heaven. The Old Testament Israelites had known all along what God wanted them to do. So why didn't they all make it to the Promised Land? (4:2)

God is already "at rest" from creating the world and everything in it. Jesus has already made it possible for human beings to join God in His rest (4:3-4). But as we have seen, if we are rebellious or disobedient, it is easy to miss out on what God has to offer (4:5). So what was the application for first-century Christians, or for Christians today? (4:6-11)

Getting Personal — *What does it mean to you that a heavenly rest is awaiting you?*

(Obviously, the references to "Today" in 3:13 and 4:7 do not refer to a specific 24-hour period of time, but rather refer to the need for immediate action. It's like hearing one of those goofy TV ads where "Supplies are limited, so act today." You know you have a limited period of time [perhaps more than 24 hours] in which to respond. Yet if you wait too long, you miss the offer entirely. God's offer of salvation is open "Today." But eventually Christ is going to return or we are going to die, and our opportunity for salvation will be gone.)

Many people have the attitude that the Bible is a pretty good book and that we really ought to listen to what God has to say—but if we don't, we will probably be forgiven for it. We take the Word of God much too lightly. Like the Old Testament Israelites, we hear and know what we're supposed to be doing, but we just don't feel like obeying all the time. What does the writer of Hebrews have to say about such a lackadaisical approach to our faith? (4:12-13)

These are a couple of ominous verses with which to end a session. But take heart. The next session picks up at this point and provides additional comfort and challenge for your spiritual development. We want to stop at this point so we can consider (with full impact) the greatness of God and all the glory of His Son, Jesus Christ. This same Jesus—who is greater than Moses, greater than the angels, greater than any other created being—is glad to call us His brothers and sisters (2:10-11). And as we bring this session to a close, we want to spend a few minutes considering how it came to be that we can so easily lay claim to being brothers and sisters of Jesus.

 JOURNEY INWARD

A lot of times people are strongly drawn to the sections in the Bible that talk about how Jesus loves them, forgives them, wants to be their friend, enables them to be co-heirs with Him to receive everything God has to offer, and so forth. All those things are true, but sometimes the same people are quick to skip over the portions of the Bible that encourage them to deny themselves, take up their crosses, suffer a little, and do what Jesus wants them to do. They want all the privileges of Christianity with none of the commitments. We all need to remember that Jesus is a lot more than our Big Buddy in the Sky. And it might help us to review the first four chapters of Hebrews and see what they suggest about the issue of **status** ("position or rank in relation to others").

First, let's consider the status of Jesus. He is the Son of God, "the radiance of God's glory and the exact representation of His being" (1:3). He is greater than Moses. He is greater than the angels. He is superior to anything or anyone we could ever imagine. And yet He willingly laid aside His status to lower Himself to our level. Because He lowered Himself, He made it possible for all of us to become His sisters and brothers — to share in everything to which He was originally entitled.

Your image of Jesus may be one of humility and submission. That's OK. During His earthly life, He was simple and (from a lot of people's viewpoints) unimpressive. Yet we should always integrate that image of Jesus with the fact that He was in on the Creation of the world and the salvation of humankind, and will be our final Judge when this world finally comes to an end. (You'll learn more about His role as Judge later in this book.)

Use this pie chart to illustrate how you perceive Jesus. The circle symbolizes His wholeness. You should draw "pieces" to show how much you think of Jesus in each of His roles. Consider these possibilities:

❏ Giver/Answerer of Prayer (G) — He provides you with all the good things you need in life.
❏ Friend (F) — He makes Himself available to you at all times, offering encouragement and help.
❏ Judge (J) — He will eventually pass judgment on the entire world.
❏ Defender (D) — He is a Mediator between you and God the Father.
❏ Savior (S) — He is the only reason you can call yourself a Christian and look forward to eternal life.
❏ Lord and Master (L/M) — He is the One who should be in complete control of your life.
❏ Rescuer (R) — He is there in times of distress and trouble, to help you through your hard situations.

❑ Other — (List as many other roles as you would like.)

Don't expect your "pie" to necessarily contain a number of equal-sized pieces. Perhaps half the time you think about Jesus, you're asking Him for something. If so, your chart might look like this. Just try to be as honest as possible.

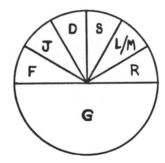

This exercise should help you see if you are giving Jesus proper consideration for all He has done (and continues to do) for you. And if we genuinely begin to comprehend what we are entitled to because Jesus gave up His status, the next logical question should be to suppose what *we* might be able to do if we weren't so concerned about our own status.

Most people seek status sometime in their lives. In high school, they may have played on sports teams or in the band. In college, they may have become officers in one of the clubs or attained some other leadership roles. At work, they maneuver in the "right" circle of friends. But very few people feel that they have enough status, and they continue to try to find ways to gain more and more recognition. So the next pie chart is for you.
Consider for a few minutes how much time you put into thinking about or working toward each of the following things. Then draw in the pieces of your pie that will include all that apply.

❑ Money (M)—Being able to afford the things you (and perhaps your family) want.

❑ Popularity (P)—The ability to attract a crowd wherever you go.

❑ Fame (F)—Awards, titles, your name in the paper once in a while, etc.

❑ Reputation (R)—Having people remember you, even when you're not around.

❑ Obedience to Jesus (O)—Conscious thought about how you can be a better Christian.

❑ Recognition at Work (W)—Being noticed by your coworkers.

❑ Personal Character (C)—Having people notice how cool you are.

This pie chart isn't to separate right from wrong. Nothing you've listed is necessarily wrong in itself. But the balance of these things is important. If you notice that you're spending a lot more time on the things that promote your level of status than you do in trying to be a better Christian, then you likely need to reconsider your priorities. If you find that you are sacrificing relationships to reach for status, remember that Jesus sacrificed status while reaching for people. And as His sisters and brothers, we should follow His example. Obedient Christians shouldn't be status seekers. They shouldn't get caught up with status symbols. For us, loyal devotion to Jesus should just be status quo.

 KEY VERSE

"The Word of God is living and active. Sharper than any double-edged sword, it penetrates even to dividing soul and spirit, joints and marrow; it judges the thoughts and attitudes of the heart. Nothing in all creation is hidden from God's sight. Everything is uncovered and laid bare before the eyes of Him to whom we must give account" (Hebrews 4:12-13).

It's difficult to feel empathy for anyone with whom we haven't shared emotions or experiences.

2

SHARE THE FEELING

(Hebrews 4:14–10:39)

Martin, I don't know how to tell you this, but I want a divorce."

"You've got to be kidding, Beth. We've only been married for two weeks."

"Seventeen long, grueling days, to be exact. In that amount of time, I've come to see very clearly that we just aren't compatible as a couple."

"But before we were married, you said I was the only guy for you."

"I thought you were, Martin. I chose you over all the rest. I thought you were special."

"So what happened?"

"I didn't know you were so . . . selfish."

"What? Me? Selfish?"

"That's right. Look at this budget you drew up. When we were dating, you gave me flowers . . . or candy . . . or *something* every week. You took me out to eat. You spent time with me. Now you're working two shifts. And where does the money go? Toward monthly payments on an expensive stereo system and a sports car. For what you've allotted for groceries, we can barely afford to have macaroni and cheese every night."

"C'mon Beth. The car and stereo are for both of us. I can't help it that we had to cut back on those other things. If *you* had a job, we could afford more."

"Go ahead! Rub it in. You know I'm looking for a job. Why don't *you* stay home and let *me* work?"

"Get real, Beth. The husband is supposed to do the work and the wife is supposed to stay home."

"Says who, you selfish—"

"Says me. Like it or not, we *are* married. And if you don't cooperate, we're going to lose everything good we have had together."

"Maybe you're right."

"And maybe you're right about the budget. I'll think about getting a cheaper car so we can afford some food. We'll talk about it tonight. OK?"

"OK."

Are you familiar with the word *empathy*? If not, it's one you should learn. According to Webster, empathy is "the capacity for participation in another's feelings or ideas." Simply put, empathy is being able to feel what someone else must be feeling.

Empathy is why some people cry at sad movies. They put themselves in the place of the characters and begin to feel the same despair. A good lawyer tries to get the jury to empathize with his client—to get them to feel the emotions that the person was feeling when he murdered his wife.

Empathy is more than mere concern. You might be concerned about the starving children in the world. You may sympathize for them. You may send them money for food. But until you sense the same hunger and desperation for yourself, you can't really empathize with them. Similarly, it's difficult to feel empathy for anyone with whom you haven't shared emotions or experiences.

JOURNEY ONWARD

Sometimes we may wonder if God really understands our plight as humans—the occasional loneliness, despair, fear, confusion, and numerous other "weaknesses." After all, He is God. Is God really able to empathize with us?

The writer of Hebrews would answer that question with a thundering yes!

You should remember from the last session that Jesus is greater than Moses, greater than the angels, and so forth. But one of the main reasons Jesus deserves such recognition and praise is the fact that He voluntarily gave up His "status" as God and willingly took on a human form. Though He never stopped being God, His humanity allowed Him to personally relate to every human emotion that we feel.

Read Hebrews 4:14-16.

In this session, Jesus is portrayed as a high priest. You may remember from your Old Testament readings that the high priest was the person responsible for representing the Israelites before God. He would enter the most holy place of the tabernacle once a year and make atonement for the people's sins. He would seek God's will on important matters and relay it to the people. He was in charge of all the worship activities that would keep the people's minds focused on God. Yet the Old Testament high priests were still human and, therefore, imperfect. But now that Jesus in all His perfection is acting as our High Priest, what should we do? (Hebrews 4:14)

What makes Jesus such a good High Priest on our behalf? (4:15)

How does Jesus' role as High Priest affect our relationship with God? (4:16)

Read Hebrews 5:1-14.
How did Jesus become our High Priest? (5:1-6)

(If the reference to Melchizedek confuses you, hold on. His name will come up again in a few minutes.)

Even when Jesus was on earth, He acted in the role of a high priest for His people. How? (5:7-10)

Milkshakes or Prime Rib?
Read Hebrews 6:1-20.
This portrayal of Jesus as a high priest isn't all that hard to understand. Yet at the time the Book of Hebrews was written, many of the people weren't trying real hard to mature in their faith. Consequently, the writer had to chide them a little bit. Using the same comparison that Paul had made to the Corinthians, this author compared his simplified teaching to "milk," when the people should have been ready for "solid food" (1 Corinthians 3:2; Hebrews 5:11-14). The writer of Hebrews then reviewed some basics that the people should have been aware of (6:1-3), and reminded them that if they weren't maturing, then they were falling away from their faith. In essence, what is the tragic consequence of someone who has become a Christian allowing himself (or herself) to "fall away" from Christian beliefs? (6:4-6)

Getting Personal — *Have you ever been tempted to "fall away" from your Christian beliefs? What prevented you from doing so?*

What illustration did the author use to symbolize the contrast between Christians who receive God's blessing and are fruitful, and Christians who receive God's blessing but ignore everything they receive? (6:7-8)

What was the writer's purpose in bringing up this touchy issue of Christians who weren't acting like Christians? (6:9-12)

In contrast to the weak faith of some of the people of his time, the writer recalled the life of Abraham. When it took a while (25 years, to be exact) for Abraham to receive the son that God had promised him, he didn't waver in his faith. He waited patiently. God swore an oath to Abraham to confirm that He would honor His promise. We can be just as sure of God's promises today because Jesus is acting in the role of our High Priest (6:13-20).

Read Hebrews 7:1-28.
At this point, the writer of Hebrews went into more detail concerning the comparisons between the priesthoods of Jesus and Melchizedek. If you want to review the appearance of Melchizedek in the Old Testament, read Genesis 14:17-20. Then review Hebrews 7:1-3 and list the ways that Melchizedek symbolized the priesthood of Jesus.

First-century Hebrew Christians reading this for the first time would have been more accustomed to the priesthood of Aaron, who descended from the tribe of Levi. But, as the writer pointed out, Melchizedek was a different — and better — kind of priest. Whereas previous tradition had held that tithes be offered to the priests descended from Levi, the writer of Hebrews explained that, in one sense, Levi offered tithes to Melchizedek. When Abraham offered a tenth of his goods to Melchizedek, he was going to have Isaac as a son who would have Jacob as a son who would have Levi as a son. So Levi was somewhere in the chromosomes of Abraham when Abraham paid tribute to Melchizedek (7:4-10).

If people only honored priests from the tribe of Levi, then Jesus couldn't qualify. He was from the tribe of Judah. But since the acceptance of Melchizedek as priest was in Old Testament Scripture, the people could see that Jesus was a priest in the same sense. Why was it necessary for a priest to arise who wasn't from the levitical priesthood? (7:11-22)

In what other ways is Jesus different from the priests who were from the tribe of Levi? (7:23-28)

Read Hebrews 8:1-13.
You might ask, "If Jesus is such a great priest, why wasn't He a *real* priest when He was on earth? Even though He fulfilled many of the duties of a priest, He didn't spend His time in the temple with the other priests. Why not?" It's a good question. How did the writer of Hebrews answer it? (8:1-6)

The writer then quoted a long passage from Jeremiah 31:31-34 detailing the events of a New Covenant God had promised to form with His people. The coming of Jesus had ushered in this New Covenant. How would things in this New Covenant differ from the Mosaic Covenant? (8:7-12)

What underlying truth can be assumed just by the fact that God has indeed made a New Covenant with His people? (8:13)

Getting Personal — *What aspects of the New Covenant are most significant to you?*

Read Hebrews 9:1-15.
In continuing his comparison between the old and new, the writer of Hebrews reminded his readers of the Old Testament tabernacle. In the outer area was a bronze altar and basin. This was where the people would bring their animal offerings to be sacrificed. An enclosed room within this area was called the Holy Place, which only priests could enter. It contained a table for the priests' consecrated bread, an altar for incense, and a lampstand—with all of the articles either pure gold or gold-covered. This

room contained an entrance to an attached, smaller room separated by a veil.

The smaller room was the Most Holy Place, which only the high priest could enter (and *he* could only go in once a year). The Most Holy Place contained the golden ark of the covenant, which symbolized God's presence among the Israelites. It was on the ark of the covenant that blood was sprinkled on the annual Day of Atonement, when the high priest would enter the Most Holy Place and make atonement (reconciliation between God and humankind) for himself, his family, and all the Israelites for another year. In the Old Testament, animals could be offered throughout the year by people seeking forgiveness for specific sins. But this Day of Atonement was the holiest day of the year.

The writer of Hebrews reminded us of this Old Testament system. He also let us know, in passing, what was contained in the ark of the covenant. What three things were inside? (9:1-5)

What was a major shortcoming of the Old Testament method of worship? (9:6-10)

Getting Personal — *Are there any shortcomings in your method of worship?*

How did Jesus improve on this system? (9:11-15)

A New and Improved Covenant
Read Hebrews 9:16-28.
Of course, it was through Jesus' death that the change from the Old to the New Covenant could be made. The Greek word for *covenant* is the same word they used for *will*, as in "last will and testament." In what respects was Jesus' New Covenant like a will? (9:16-18)

Jesus' New Covenant was similar to the old one in that both required the shedding of blood before the people's sins could be forgiven. But the tabernacle was just a "copy" of what God had intended. When an architect is about to construct a large building, he will usually design a scale model before he starts so his client can see exactly what the finished product will look like. The tabernacle, with its wooden frame, curtains, gold and bronze furnishings, and so forth, was a symbolic model for a flesh-and-blood replacement who would atone for sin and bring together God and humans. Obviously, the tabernacle had been man-made. How then was Jesus' New Covenant superior to the Old Covenant? List all the differences you can find (9:18-28).

In addition to being a "copy" of the real thing (9:24), what other illustration is made to describe the Old Testament approach to forgiveness of sins? (10:1)

Read Hebrews 10:1-39.
A lot of emphasis should be placed on the fact that Jesus' sacrifice (the shedding of His blood) was "once for all" (9:26). What had people come to realize from having to offer animal sacrifices for their sins year after year? (10:1-4)

God had never wanted piles of slaughtered animals from His people. The whole concept of Old Testament animal offerings was for the benefit of the people, not God. Only by repeatedly seeing the severity of bloodshed could people begin to understand God's ultimate level of love in allowing His only Son to undergo that same process for us (10:5-10).

Getting Personal—*How do you respond to the sight of bloodshed?*

What do you think is significant about the fact that the earthly priests are portrayed as "standing" while Jesus is described as "sitting"? (10:11-12)

What is Jesus waiting for? (10:13-18)

As you have seen, the author has gone into considerable detail about the past history of Jewish worship. You probably already knew many of the facts he reviewed. And certainly his first-century readers would have known most of these things. But this review was necessary for what he was leading up to. Because we are living under the "new and improved" priesthood of Jesus, we are encouraged to *do* three things and to *not do* one specific thing. What are those four specific actions? (10:19-25)

How serious should we be in responding to the facts in this section of Hebrews? Explain (10:26-31).

At this point, the issue of empathy becomes important. Jesus modeled empathy when He became a human and went through numerous experiences He shouldn't have been subjected to. But His motive was love. As we follow His example, we should do the same thing. How had the first-century Christians been showing empathy for each other? (10:32-34)

Getting Personal — *How would you evaluate your own ability to show empathy?*

But many of these people were falling away from their faith. What reasons did the writer of Hebrews give them to keep holding on to what they believed? (10:35-39)

The next session will provide some additional reasons for remaining faithful as we get to the "big finish" of the Book of Hebrews. But before we move on, let's stop and apply what we've discovered so far.

 JOURNEY INWARD

The Book of Hebrews gives us a unique picture of Jesus Christ. What we saw in the last session was nothing really new: He is greater than Moses, greater than the angels, and so forth. Yet from this session you might begin to think of Him in a new way—as a heavenly High Priest who intercedes to God on your behalf. And the thing that makes Him such an effective High Priest is that He has gone through every bit of pain and suffering involved with being human. Because of what He has done for us, He has a lot to teach us about **empathy.**

Jesus has already put Himself in your place, so try for a moment to put yourself in His place. Suppose you had spent every moment of eternity in the presence of God. By the way, you have always existed. "Time" is a concept that doesn't apply to you. You have never sinned. You are perfect in every way. You have a loving relationship with God your Father in heaven and have all the angels giving you praise. And then, according to God's plan, you are sent to earth to live as a human being for about 33 years. Imagine this had been your situation, and answer the following questions:

❑ Do you think you would have been willing to go to earth? Explain.

❏ Knowing what you do about Jesus' life, what do you think would have been the best part of your life on earth?

❏ What would have been the worst part?

❏ What things might you have done differently than Jesus?

It is likely that you find it a little hard to put yourself in the place of Jesus. But it's important to remember that He had the same emotions (love, compassion, anger) that you have. He had the same physical weaknesses (hunger, weariness, pain). He suffered the same hurts (betrayal, rejection, mockery). And it is exactly because He endured all these things that He can now be an effective advocate for us before God.

While we may not be able to empathize with Jesus, we should at least try to empathize with each other. Many of the problems we experience as Christians are due to a lack of empathy. How many times do you argue with your children without even trying to put yourself in their place? How many times do you hastily pass judgment on someone else when you know little, if anything, about that person's situation? How many of your relationships would instantly become stronger if you would put yourself in the other person's shoes?

Think through your actions of the past week, or perhaps the past month. Then make two lists. On the first list, put the names of all the people for whom you think you should try to feel more empathy. On the second list, place the names of all the people you wish would try to know you better. (You may have some of the same names on both lists.)

I Should Show More Empathy For These People	These People Should Show More Empathy For Me

Now for the hard part: You need to select a couple of people from your first list and conduct an informal interview with them. Find out what their interests are. If you already know, then concentrate more on their inner thoughts and dreams. Be friendly.

With the people on your second list, you may need to be more open. This is true for coworkers, children, casual acquaintances, or even best friends. If you are afraid to be vulnerable with the people close to you, then they can never really know you.

Some of these confrontations may be a little uncomfortable for you at first. But remember that Jesus' sacrificial action was necessary for the good of God's kingdom. In much the same way, any sacrifice you make for the good of someone else will also benefit the kingdom of God. Give it some thought, and then give it some action.

 KEY VERSE

"We do not have a high priest who is unable to sympathize with our weaknesses, but we have one who has been tempted in every way, just as we are—yet was without sin. Let us then approach the throne of grace with confidence, so that we may receive mercy and find grace to help us in our time of need" (Hebrews 4:15-16).

Hey, how did that guy ever make the list?!

3

PEERS LOOKING AT YOU, KID

(Hebrews 11–13)

Just about every year some magazine polls a number of people to find out whom they most admire. The magazine then publishes a "Top Ten" list in one of its issues and the readers sit around and say, "Yeah, good answer," or, "No way, man. How did that guy ever make it on this list?"

One of the big problems with such polls is that the number of people questioned is usually small, and only a minority of people get to express themselves. So here's your opportunity. For each of the following categories, try to come up with the one person (or two at the most) that you admire more than anyone else.

❏ Actor/Actress —

❏ Business figure —

❏ Sports figure —

❏ Book character —

❏ Comic strip character —

❏ Musician or music group —

❏ Politician —

And on a more personal level, try these categories:

❑ Coworker —

❑ Relative —

❑ Church member —

❑ Friend —

What other people do you admire that might not have been included in any of the previous categories?

In the magazine polls, the results usually include the people you might expect: the current President, some of the hottest actors, a couple of big sports heroes, some musicians, and so forth. Often the polls will also include the Pope, Billy Graham, or some other leading religious figure. The magazines don't usually analyze their lists. They provide the information and move on to the next article.

But as you review your own list of people, think of how you may be influenced by each individual you've mentioned. Such influence won't be direct in most cases. It's not as if listing Michael Jordan will automatically make you a better basketball player, but it may explain why you spend more time on the basketball court than you do bowling, playing volleyball, or involved in some other sport you enjoy. Your musical preference may suggest that you have adopted certain opinions and attitudes. On the other hand, the people you select might reflect an inner admiration for humility and gentleness. (That is, if you opted for Helen Keller instead of Wanda the Warrior Woman Wrestler.)

You sometimes hear about the dangers of hero worship, or paying too much reverence to someone else. Yet while we definitely should avoid hero worship, there is nothing wrong with seeking mentors and selecting positive role models to imitate. In fact, we are commanded to choose our "heroes" carefully when it comes to our spiritual development.

JOURNEY ONWARD

So far the Book of Hebrews has placed most of its emphasis on the character of Jesus. Obviously, all this material is provided with the intention of having the reader put his or her faith in Jesus, our High Priest and King. But at this point, we are challenged to consider exactly what faith is. We are given an explanation both by definition and by example.

Read Hebrews 11:1-3.
Perhaps you've heard a lot of people speak of the importance of faith. But often "faith" seems like some vague, undefined concept that is difficult to envision and put into practice. The writer of Hebrews, however, provides a clear, concise definition. What is faith? (Hebrews 11:1)

Not only is faith defined for us, it will also be illustrated time and time again. For example, what is one way that faith increases our understanding of God? (11:3)

Getting Personal—*Who is the greatest person of faith that you have ever known?*

Faith Hall of Fame
Read Hebrews 11:4-34.
Faith also increased the understanding of God for many Old Testament characters (11:2). What follows in this section of Hebrews is sometimes referred to as the Faith Hall of Fame. As you read through the names and accomplishments of each person listed here, first jot down a phrase or so to help you remember why he or she stood out in the area of faith. Then make another note to help identify characteristics or facts about faith that stand out in the person's life. The following chart will help you organize your thoughts. (Some of the following references are short. And if you need to review some of these stories, an Old Testament reference is also included for you to consult.)

Person/Event	Significant Accomplishment(s)	What You Can Learn About Faith
Abel Hebrews 11:4 Genesis 4:1-12		
Enoch Hebrews 11:5-6 Genesis 5:21-24		
Noah Hebrews 11:7 Genesis 6		
Abraham (1st example) Hebrews 11:8-10 Genesis 12–15		
Abraham (2nd example) Hebrews 11:11-16 Genesis 16–21		
Abraham (3rd example) Hebrews 11:17-19 Genesis 22:1-19		
Isaac Hebrews 11:20 Genesis 27		
Jacob Hebrews 11:21 Genesis 48		
Joseph Hebrews 11:22 Genesis 50:22-26		
Moses' parents Hebrews 11:23 Exodus 1:1–2:10		
Moses Hebrews 11:24-28 Exodus 2:11–12:51		
People of Israel (1st example) Hebrews 11:29 Exodus 14		

Person/Event	Significant Accomplishment(s)	What You Can Learn About Faith
People of Israel (2nd example) Hebrews 11:30 Joshua 6		
Rahab Hebrews 11:31 Joshua 2; 6:22-25		

Let's pause for a moment and consider what you've learned so far. Even though the previous chart is somewhat lengthy, try not to rush through it. Tucked away in these verses are some remarkable insights. For example, did you notice that Abraham had such faith that he could expect God to resurrect his son, Isaac—even though Abraham had never even heard of a dead person being raised before? (Hebrews 11:19) It's incredible to think that someone could cling so tightly to a promise of God that he would naturally expect God to perform so great a miracle, if necessary.

Another thing you may have noticed is that several of the people mentioned are remembered for "minor" things. Isaac, Jacob, and Joseph, for example, all had more breathtaking experiences to recall than passing along God's blessing to their children and grandchildren. But the emphasis here in Hebrews 11 is on "being sure of what we hope for and certain of what we do not see." God's promise to Abraham of the establishment of a great nation was passed down through Isaac, Jacob, and Jacob's children. Though it took many years for the covenant to be fulfilled, these key people are remembered because they continued to look ahead and expected God to fulfill His promises.

Finally, consider the wide assortment of people listed here. We expect to see people like Abraham, Noah, and Moses. Of course they deserve to be in this Hall of Fame. But we also find Abel, who is remembered for the sincere offering he made to God. We find Enoch, of whom we know little except that "he walked with God." And we find Rahab the prostitute, whose faith allowed her and her family to escape the otherwise complete destruction of Jericho. It seems that anyone can qualify for the Faith Hall of Fame if he or she is only willing to let go and trust God completely. God doesn't expect everyone to be a "superstar" like Abraham, Noah, and Moses. As the Hall of Fame listing continues, we are reminded of the faith of Gideon (Judges 6–8), Barak (Judges 4), Samson (Judges 13–16), Jephthah (Judges 11), David

(1 Samuel 16–1 Kings 2), Samuel (1 Samuel 1–16), and the prophets. If you don't recognize all of these names, you may want to go back and review their stories.

The emphasis then shifts from the names of people to the accomplishments for which many of them are remembered. For each accomplishment listed in Hebrews 11:33-35, match it with the person who might have been referred to (though many of the statements could apply to more than one person).

Conquered kingdoms	Daniel (Daniel 6)
Administered justice and gained what was promised	Joshua (Joshua 10:40-42)
Shut the mouths of lions	Elisha (2 Kings 4:32-37)
Quenched the fury of the flames	David (2 Samuel 5:1-5)
Escaped the edge of the sword	Solomon (1 Kings 3:28; 4:20-21)
Weakness was turned to strength	Elijah (1 Kings 19)
Became powerful in battle and routed foreign armies	Shadrach, Meshach, Abednego (Daniel 3)
Woman received back her dead, raised to life again.	Samson (Judges 16:20-30)

It's Not All Peaches and Cream
Read Hebrews 11:35-40.
Up to this point, faith sounds like a lot of fun—conquering kingdoms, acquiring power, experiencing death-defying narrow escapes, and such. But true faith doesn't always have such happy results. What other consequences did God's faithful people encounter? (Hebrews 11:35-38)

Getting Personal—*Has your faith caused you to encounter any negative consequences?*

We usually tend to think that the actions these people took are why they are considered so faithful. But their actions become even more noteworthy in light of one significant fact. Why else do all these Old Testament characters deserve special honor? (11:39)

And while they should all be important to us, we are likewise important to them. Why? (11:40)

Read Hebrews 12:1-29.
As we think about all these outstanding role models, what actions should we begin to take? (12:1-2)

Getting Personal — *What are some obstacles that hinder you in your race?*

As we develop our faith, we are supposed to look backward to the Old Testament heroes and heroines whose actions have been recorded for our encouragement. We are to recall Jesus' painful and humiliating sacrifice on the cross. But we are also to look ahead, keeping our eyes on the resurrected Jesus, who is now with God the Father. If we keep all these things in mind, what will be the result? (12:3)

Most people don't enjoy any form of discomfort. One extreme type of difficulty arises from taking such a firm stand against sin that your blood is shed. In a nation that allows for religious freedom, we are not usually confronted with such extremes. But at the other extreme is the problem of refusing to stand against sin at all. When this becomes the case, sometimes we encounter a different kind of difficulty—the discipline of God. Some of the hardships we experience are actually God's attempts to nudge us back toward Him. And while we may not enjoy such hardships, we should appreciate them. Why? (12:4-10)

When we undergo the discipline of God and are willing to learn from it, what do we stand to gain? (12:11-12)

As we respond to God's discipline, how should our personal relationships be affected? (12:13-17)

(Notice that a negative role model is included for consideration at this point. Just as we can learn from the good lessons of Abraham, Isaac, and Jacob, we can also benefit from many of the Old Testament stories that didn't have a happy ending.)

Getting Personal — *Is there anyone with whom you are not living in peace?*

After we realize that God's discipline is a result of His love for us, we should have a different outlook pertaining to our worship habits. In God's dealings with Moses and the Israelites, what was the mood when God spoke to His people? (12:18-21; also Exodus 19:10-25)

God no longer speaks to us from a literal Mount Sinai. Rather, He resides in heaven, symbolized by Mount Zion. But His message is no less important now than it was then. So how are we to respond to Him? (Hebrews 12:22-29)

Read Hebrews 13:1-25.
As the Book of Hebrews draws to a close, the author makes a number of challenges to his readers. Why does he say it's important to be nice to strangers who need help? (13:1-2)

To what extent should we be concerned about friends in prison (or otherwise suffering)? (13:3)

How essential is it to be loyal in marriage? (13:4)

What should be our attitude toward money? (13:5-6)

What should be our relationship to our spiritual leaders? (13:7-17)

Getting Personal—*In which of the above areas do you need to work the most? In which are you strongest?*

In the benediction of the book, what was the author's wish for his readers? (13:20-21)

 JOURNEY INWARD

This section of Hebrews can give us a new perspective on the importance of selecting **role models.** More than likely, your list at the beginning of this session didn't include any of the people listed in the Faith Hall of Fame. It's not often that we sit back and think, *Wow! That Enoch was quite a guy. I should be more like him.*

Too often we single out heroes who fall far short of these biblical standards. Many of our sports favorites have short tempers and unrepeatable vocabularies. And it seems like every time you get to liking a politician, he or she is suddenly confronted by the media with some previously hidden scandal.

Yet in spite of the shortcomings of our current heroes, we probably spend more time admiring them than we do in remembering the "great cloud of witnesses" spoken of in Hebrews. And if we aren't careful, we may begin to absorb some of the bad influences as well as the good from the lives of the people we have chosen as role models.

In the space below, copy the names of all the people you listed as role models at the first of this session. Think about each of your choices, and then beside each name note any of that person's characteristics that you *don't* want to imitate. You may not come up with anything for some of them, but you'll probably think of something in most cases. Even if you've listed parents or close friends you really admire, you're probably aware of a trait or two that you would try to avoid. In other instances, you may not know enough about the person to list anything. But fill in as many as you can.

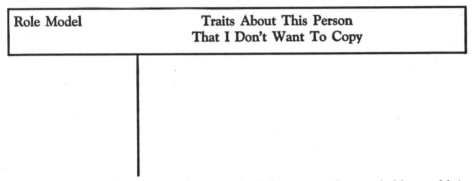

Role Model	Traits About This Person That I Don't Want To Copy

Now review your list again. This time look for names that probably wouldn't have been there a year ago. List them below.

You will probably notice that the list of people you most admire tends to change fairly regularly. By this time next year, your list will probably undergo another major change. From what you've observed so far, you may have noticed several things about role models. Add your comments to those listed below.

(1) *We all tend to look up to certain people.* It's a natural human response to want to be like people we admire. There's nothing wrong in noticing positive qualities in other people and trying to integrate those qualities into our own lives. Yet we must be careful not to ignore our own distinct personalities in trying so hard to be like someone else.

(2) *We should be very selective when choosing role models.* It's easy to like someone so much that we begin to imitate everything he or she does—both good and bad. Since musicians, sports figures, politicians, etc., can quickly rise and fall in popularity polls, we should try to choose role models based on their behavior over a lengthy period of time.

(3) *Some role models deserve more of our attention than others.* Most of the current role models we choose will pale next to those listed in Hebrews 11. True, none of the biblical examples were perfect either. They were all sinful human beings. But they never allowed themselves to stray too far from God's leading.

(4) *Jesus should be the #1 role model for every Christian.* This statement should go without saying. Yet to be truthful, most of us probably spend a whole lot more time trying to look like, play like, sing like, or otherwise be like the people on magazine covers than we do trying to be like Jesus. We would do better for ourselves to get to know Jesus and then imitate His perfection.

(5) *You are a role model.* Perhaps you missed this truth. But a lot of eyes are on you. You have a lot of influence on your family and friends. If you have qualities that they like, they'll actually try to be more like you (though they might not admit it). So your goal for the next week or so should be to try to imagine that everyone is looking at you all the time. Act as if every movement might be copied by someone you care a lot about. (If you're imitating Jesus, you'll be fine. But if not. . . .)

You may never make it into anyone's Role Model Hall of Fame. But just *trying* to be a good role model will probably teach you things about yourself that may surprise you. And when it gets tough to live a life worth imitating, take a hint from the author of Hebrews: Have faith!

 KEY VERSE

"*Without faith it is impossible to please God, because anyone who comes to Him must believe that He exists and that He rewards those who earnestly seek Him*" (Hebrews 11:6).

Taming the tongue is no easy task.

4

WORD PERFECT

(Book of James)

M onday morning at 5 o'clock, the blare of Melinda's alarm signaled the beginning of another day. And as usual, the first words out of her mouth weren't appropriate to be repeated verbatim. Let's just say that they summarized her displeasure at having to get up while it was still cold and dark outside. But an hour and a half later—after a hot shower, a hairstyling, a manicure, and the application of a vast assortment of miracle cosmetics, Melinda was ready to begin another week. She took one last glance in the mirror and said to herself, "Perfect! *Now* you're starting to look like your true self. Nobody's going to give *you* any serious competition, you good-looking woman."

She then took a quick walk through the kitchen to get a piece of toast for breakfast. When her roommate prodded her to sit down and eat something else, she said, "Don't worry. I'll eat something later" (knowing full well she would have the usual—potato chips and a chocolate shake).

At work, she saw her boss, Mr. Elwood, with his usual Monday-morning-who-knows-what-shade-of-green-it-is sports coat. But since raise time was nearing, she said, "Hi, Mr. Elwood. You're looking sharp this morning." He gave her a look that suggested he knew exactly what she thought of him and just kept walking.

In the office, Melinda and her friends couldn't wait to catch up on each other's weekend gossip. "Did you hear about Mary?" "No, what happened to her?" "I hear she and Dense Dave were at the clinic this weekend!" "No kidding? Why?" "My guess is they're in serious trouble and getting blood tests."

At that moment Mary rounded the corner, looked Melinda straight in the eye, and said, "Are you talking about me?" The room was deathly silent until Melinda said in her perkiest voice, "No way. Kim, uh, wanted a present for her boyfriend and I said, uh, 'Go to Sears . . . on the double . . . they're the best.' " Of course, Mary didn't believe it, but Melinda and her friends had a good laugh.

Melinda isn't really a bad person. In fact, if you knew her, you'd probably like her. She's a little high-spirited, but not unlike most other women her age. Yet her "little" faults reveal two common denominators—lack of thought and an uncontrollable tongue. In this short introduction, you've seen her boast, lie, swear, gossip, use flattery, call people names, break promises, slander, and use sarcasm. And most of these offenses were committed without thinking. So you see, she's not that much different than all the rest of us.

 JOURNEY ONWARD

Let's turn our attention from Melinda to a man named James. We're likely to learn a little more from James' examples than from Melinda's.

The New Testament refers to more than one person named James. Most people agree that the writer of this book was not James the apostle, because he died so early (Acts 12:1-2). Rather, it is believed that this James was one of Jesus' brothers. (Technically, it would be more accurate to call him a half brother, since James' parents were Mary and Joseph while Jesus was conceived by the Spirit of God.)

The Book of James is like an instruction manual in many ways. Perhaps you've tried to assemble something without reading the instructions, only to become bewildered and irritated. When you finally look at the instructions, you often discover that you only made a tiny mistake, but one that cost you a lot of wasted time and effort. Whenever your Christian life seems to be getting out of balance, James is a good book to consult. It's short, easy to read and understand, and filled with helpful information and worthwhile challenges. And it's likely to reveal what might be wrong in your life and get you back on track.

Read James 1:1-21.
Even though the author was physically close to Jesus while growing up, he didn't believe in Him at first (John 7:5). But later James became a key figure in the development of the early church. You might think that he would play up his kinship to Jesus if he wanted people to pay attention to him. But as he opened his book, what does he say his relationship was to Jesus? (James 1:1)

Also notice to whom James addresses his book—the 12 tribes scattered among the nations. As you read through what he has to say, keep in mind that James is writing primarily to Jewish Christians under persecution. James knew these people were suffering. What did he want them to do about it? Why? (1:2-4)

Getting Personal—*Which is harder for you—going through a tough time yourself, or watching someone you care about go through a trial?*

Obviously James' advice might have prompted the reply: "That's easy for him to say. But just *how* are we supposed to do what he says?" How did James answer that reasonable question? (1:5)

Then James revealed the secret of why we often don't get what we ask God for. What sometimes keeps us from having good, open communication with God? (1:5-8)

If God seems to have blessed some people more than others with material possessions and recognition, how should people respond who don't have much? (1:9)

51

Getting Personal — *Do you consider yourself blessed? Why or why not?*

How about the people who are doing pretty well? (1:10-11)

What is in store for people who persevere under unpleasant circumstances? (1:12)

Many people who don't persevere try to blame God for their failure. Why is that the wrong thing to do? (1:13-15)

What things do we need to keep in mind about God? (1:16-18)

What things do we need to keep in mind about relating to each other? (1:19-21)

If you've been paying close attention, you may have noticed that James hasn't hit us with any drastically earthshaking information yet. Most of what he says is just good common sense: Bear up during difficult times. Ask God for help when you need it. Don't be a wimpy Christian. Don't take comfort in the amount of money you have. Don't blame God when *you* mess up your life. Get along with God. Get along with each other.

Yet so often, it is one (or more) of these simple truths we have ignored that causes us grief as Christians. We need to reread James' "instruction manual" from time to time as a checklist to help us know what to do. Yet just *knowing* what to do isn't enough.

The Spiritual Mirror

When you get up in the morning, one of the first things you probably do is look in a mirror. You see those disgusting blobs of whatever that stuff is in the corners of your eyes. You observe the residue from where you were drooling in your sleep again last night. And we won't even mention your hair. As you look at yourself, you can see exactly what you need to do. At that point, do you just leave the house the way you are? Or do you jump into action to try to patch yourself together as best you can?

Read James 1:22-27.
James uses a similar example to demonstrate the need for action—not just knowledge—in our Christian lives. What is our spiritual "mirror," and why is it essential that we look into it on a regular basis? (1:22-25)

Specifically, what are a few actions we need to take to demonstrate our Christian beliefs? (1:26-27)

Getting Personal—*Who are the needy in your community? What are you doing to minister to them?*

Read James 2:1-26.
James continued his common-sense advice with a discussion on favoritism. It's never good when Christians play favorites—for any reason. But in a church setting, it is particularly harmful to show more attention to rich people than poorer ones (2:1-4). It's also kind of stupid. Why? (2:5-7)

Everyone knows that murder and adultery are sins and would expect to be punished for such offenses. Showing favoritism is also a sin, yet it is one we often overlook in others and take part in ourselves (2:8-11). Instead of needing to be judged for improper actions, what is a better alternative? (2:12-13)

When Paul wrote the Ephesians, he told them, "It is by grace you have been saved, through faith ... not by works" (Ephesians 2:8-9). But here James said, "Faith by itself, if it is not accompanied by action, is dead" (James 2:17). Do you think these two statements concerning faith and actions (works) are contradictory? Explain.

We need to remember to whom James was writing his book as we consider his comments on the relationship of faith and works. He is addressing Jewish Christians—people who would have been familiar with the Scripture and to whom religion had been important throughout their lives. On the other hand, the church at Ephesus (Paul's readers) probably contained a great many people who were new to Christianity and worship of the true God. So was Paul correct in telling them that Jesus' salvation was free and had no connection to the amount of work they put into it? Sure he was. And was James within his rights to tell his audience of God-fearing Jewish Christians that God expected them to back up their *words* of faith with some *actions* of faith? Of course! So our actions (our "works") have nothing to do with our *coming* to Jesus. (We can never do enough to "earn" salvation.) But our actions have a great deal to do with *living* for Jesus. When people hear that we are Christians, they are going to look at our lives to see what's so different about us. If they don't see us performing Christlike actions, we are at fault for misrepresenting what Christianity is all about.

Are there different levels of "belief" in God? Explain (James 2:18-19).

Getting Personal—*How would you describe your faith? Intellectual? Practical? Inward?*

James closed this part of his discussion by recalling two examples: Abraham's offering of his son, Isaac, and Rahab's aid to the Israelite spies (2:20-26). Both are good demonstrations of people who first said they believed, and then acted on the basis of that belief.

The Little Source of Big Problems
Read James 3:1-18.
What is the secret to leading a perfect Christian life? (3:1-2)

What other examples did James give of small things that control much larger things? (3:3-4)

See how easy this secret is! All we have to do is never say anything rotten to anyone, and we'll be just about perfect. But James knew it was no simple matter to control our words. To what did he compare a person's tongue? Why? (3:5-6)

Getting Personal — *When was the last time your tongue got you into trouble?*

Did James really expect everyone to start controlling all of their words and demonstrating Christian perfection? (3:7-8)

What is one of the worst offenses we commit with our words? (3:9-12)

A lot of what we say might come under the category of "smarting off." We think it's pretty clever to come up with good insults, names for people we don't like, put-downs, and so forth. But this kind of "wisdom" isn't what God has in mind for His people. If we have God's kind of wisdom, what will come through in our speech and our actions? (3:13-18)

Read James 4:1-17.
James then shifted from our actions to our motives. He said something to the effect of, "Come on, be honest. What really causes most of the conflicts you face?" How did he answer his own question? (4:1-3)

James encouraged us to choose friendship with God over friendship with worldly things (4:4-6). There is no middle ground. God's standards are in no way the same as the ones honored by the world system. If we choose God, what things must we do? (4:7-12)

The previous verses referred to one sin of the tongue: slander (speaking untrue things to damage someone's reputation). The next passage refers to another verbal sin: boasting. But James had a definition of boasting that may differ from the one you're familiar with. How might someone be a boaster without realizing it, and how can you avoid developing such a problem? (4:13-17)

Read James 5:1-20.
James has already warned us against showing preference to rich people while mistreating poor people. Now he addressed rich people who abuse others just because they are able to. What kind of future can they expect if they continue to choose money over God? (5:1-5)

When Christians suffer because of what mean people do to them, they have two options, one positive and one negative. What are the options and the results of each one? (5:6-11)

Another verbal sin that James addressed is our tendency to swear—not to use profanity, but to "swear to God," "swear on my mother's grave," or whatever. Many times people whose truthfulness is often questioned will begin to use such phrases when they want to emphasize that they aren't lying (this time). And usually they feel the need to use the phrase so often that it becomes automatic. You may know people who "swear to God" so many times a day that they don't even realize when they are saying it. As Christians, we shouldn't have to swear to what we are saying. What's a better habit for us to develop? (5:12)

After everything James has said about improper uses of our words, he left us with several positive goals for our speech. Review James 5:13-20 and list all of the beneficial verbal habits we should be developing.

With these verses, James wrapped up his book. He didn't beat around the bush on what he wanted to say. His thoughts are simple (yet profound) and he presents them clearly. Don't let this one session be the only time you inspect what James had to say. Come back later and spend some more time. You'll be glad you did.

 JOURNEY INWARD

James talked about a lot of worthwhile topics—temptation, prejudice, suffering, faith and actions, wisdom, submission to God, and more. But we want to focus on one specific area that James hit pretty hard—**the use of our words.** James may be correct in saying that, "No man can tame the tongue" (3:8), but that doesn't mean we aren't supposed to try. So take a few minutes to think about your speech habits. Use the following charts to help consider how much change you need to make in your use (or misuse) of words.

Let's start with the bad stuff. For each of the following misuses of your words, put a √ in the column that indicates how often you are guilty of such an offense.

	Frequently	Occasionally	Seldom	Never
Boasting (4:16)				
Lying (3:14)				
Using Profanity (3:9)				
Flattery (3:17)				
Gossip (3:16)				
Name-calling/insults (3:18)				
Oaths (swearing to God, etc.) (5:12)				
Sarcastic language (5:12)				
Slander (4:11)				
Grumbling (5:9)				

You can probably think of other categories where your words occasionally cause problems for you or someone else. But these are some common areas of word abuse. Now use the same method to determine how often your words are used for beneficial purposes.

	Frequently	Occasionally	Seldom	Never
Praise to build others up (3:9)				
Singing for God's glory (5:13)				
Truthfulness (3:14; 5:12)				
Prayer (5:13)				
Loving confrontation (5:19-20)				
Teaching (3:1-2)				
Confession (5:16)				

Perhaps you have noticed by now that there is a fine line between some of the positive and negative uses of words. For example, flattery is deceitful. But giving genuine praise is something that we are commanded to do. So we could actually use the same words, and it would be our attitudes that determine whether we are doing good or evil.

This week try to recall the worst offenses you noted on your first list. Whenever you're tempted to respond in a negative way, try to think of a positive way to reply instead. (Keeping your mouth shut may be a good way to start.) With time, you can learn to control that hyperactive tongue of yours. Enough said?

KEY VERSE

"Everyone should be quick to listen, slow to speak and slow to become angry, for man's anger does not bring about the righteous life that God desires" (James 1:19-20).

Ever had a guest who didn't know when to leave?

5

JUST PASSING THROUGH

(Book of 1 Peter)

Rick had had it. No more! No way! As soon as Rob got back from wherever he was this time, they were going to have it out. Who would have thought a year ago that anything could ever come between these two friends.

Last year when they both taught at a northern Minnesota high school, they spent lots of time together. And when Rick took a job at a school in the Florida Keys, he couldn't imagine finding another close friend like Rob. But as he started his new position and made new friends, he had to admit that his life was as good as it had ever been.

Rob, on the other hand, hadn't really tried to fill the void in his life. His teaching job just wasn't "fun" for him, so he eventually quit. Finally, he had invited himself to visit Rick in southern Florida "for a couple of days." Rick could remember his own fateful words: "I'm glad you could come, Rob. Stay as long as you like. My apartment is your apartment, so make yourself at home." That was three and a half weeks ago, and it seemed like Rob was going to be a permanent addition.

Rob had definitely made himself at home. He stayed up almost all night watching old movies (at high volume) and slept till noon. Rob didn't seem to notice the bags that were starting to form under Rick's eyes. Nor did Rob seem to notice how much he ate. An intense gravitational pull seemed to draw every scrap of food into that black hole Rob called a mouth.

And if that weren't bad enough, Rob also seemed to expect Rick to pick up after him. He left a trail of dirty dishes wherever he went. Of course, his dishes weren't always easy to find underneath all his candy wrappers, banana peels, apple cores, and empty bottles.

Rob also started wearing Rick's clothes (including his underwear!), using Rick's CD player without returning his CDs to their cases, driving Rick's car to who-knows-where, and had even begun tagging along on Rick's dates. Yet he seemed terribly offended whenever Rick would do anything with one of his new friends rather than choose to sit around and do nothing at home with his old buddy.

But the thing that had Rick really steamed this time was the note he found from Rob: "Dear Rick: I'm out of a few things, which I've included on the attached list. Could you pick them up for me? Also, could you please not make so much noise when you leave for work in the mornings? You've woken me up a couple of times—showering, eating breakfast, etc. And hey, I have some good news. I've decided to stay another couple of weeks. Great, huh? And if you could have those things for me tonight, I'd appreciate it. Thanks." Attached to the note was a two-page list that included deodorant, pork rinds, stamps, and numerous other personal (and generally unnecessary) items. Of course, Rob had left no money. And the creep was out in Rick's car, leaving no way for Rick to get out and get the stuff—even if he wanted to. At this point, Rick began to make mental notes and lists of his own, and he prepared to hit Rob full force with them the next chance he got. And first on his list was a stop at the bus station to get that moocher a ticket out of town!

You've probably had some experience of your own with guests who got a little too comfortable and didn't know when to leave. And while no one would deny that it's fun to visit new places or old friends, it's also important to remember where you really belong.

 JOURNEY ONWARD

The Book of 1 Peter is a refresher course to remind Christians where we really belong (from a spiritual perspective). Sometimes we tend to get too comfortable with life on earth, and we begin to think and act as if we belonged here. Peter's frank reminder is that we belong to God, and that our focus should be a heavenly one. Earth is just our temporary home, and we should take care not to get too attached. Otherwise we aren't much better off than Rob was in the opening story.

But we must also avoid the other extreme. Some people refer to this problem as being "so heavenly minded that you're no earthly good." If someone from another country went to your town and started ridiculing you for the way you talk, the way you act, the way you dress, and so forth, you would probably not like the person too much. Similarly, you don't want to "flaunt" your Christianity so much that you make yourself unlikable and unreachable for people who are still very much earthly minded.

As you go through the Book of 1 Peter, you will see both of these extremes addressed. The author of this book is the Peter who was Jesus' disciple. His secular fisherman background gave him a lot of experience with earthy people, and his time spent with Jesus and in the early church gave him a good perspective on spiritual things. So he had a good balanced viewpoint as he presented the type of lifestyle that heavenly minded people should have while living on earth.

Read 1 Peter 1:1-16.
Peter didn't take long getting to his point either. He addressed his writing to God's elect (or chosen people). How did he refer to these people of God? (1 Peter 1:1)

Getting Personal — *Have you ever considered yourself as "chosen" by God?*

He also said that these people were chosen through the "sanctifying work of the Spirit" (1:2). Remember that the concept of sanctification involves the "setting apart" of people for God's use. So while we are located on earth, our loyalty and purpose should be toward heaven.

Peter explained that our sanctification has come through a "new birth" that results in at least two very special benefits. What are these two things? (1:3-5)

Until the "last time," what can we expect—and why? (1:6-7)

What is the goal of faith? (1:8-9)

God had planned to accomplish this goal for many years. What people did He use, and what motivated them? (1:10-12)

Because God has done so much for us, in what ways should we be responding? (1:13-16)

Don't Get Too Comfortable
Read 1 Peter 1:17-25.
Peter's challenge to "be holy" (1:15) means to be set apart from common (earthly) things. The idea is similar to Jesus' description of our being in the world, but not of the world (John 17:15-16). So Peter began to explain how we can do just that. Yes, we are to live as strangers and not get too comfortable with an earthly lifestyle. But our attitudes are equally important. What should be a Christian's attitude while biding time here on earth? (1 Peter 1:17)

Why should we have that attitude? (1:18-19)

How long ago had God planned for Jesus to redeem humankind? (1:20-21)

And how far into the future will God's Word hold up? (1:22-25)

Read 1 Peter 2:1-25.
It's not too hard to say we should be set apart from the rest of the world. It's much harder, however, to back our words with actions (as we learned from James in the last session). So what are some common earthly habits we need to get rid of? (2:1)

What are we to crave instead? And explain what you think Peter meant by his statement (2:2-3).

Peter used a couple of phrases to describe Christians. The phrases indicated that Christians should be working together toward the same purposes. List the terms Peter used and explain what you think he meant by each one (2:4-5).

Peter referred to Jesus as the cornerstone of Christianity. People can respond to that "stone" in a couple of different ways. What are those two ways? What determines a person's response? What are the results of each response? (2:6-8)

What additional phrases did Peter use at this point to describe God's people? (2:9)

As God's people, what should we be doing? Why? (2:9-10)

Getting Personal — *Can you relate to all the descriptions of God's people in verses 9-10?*

Obviously, if we do as Peter instructed, we're likely to stand out from the people we hang around with who aren't Christians. Peter even admitted that we will likely be accused of doing wrong. But how can we turn such accusations into positive experiences? (2:11-12)

Since we are "aliens and strangers" in this world, what are some common-sense rules to live by? (2:15-17)

What should we do when someone in authority really gets on our case about something? Why? (2:18-25)

Getting Personal — *What authorities are over you?*

Read 1 Peter 3:1-14.

The boss/servant relationship isn't the only place where it's important to be different from the rest of the world. In fact, all of our relationships should reflect the fact that we're more concerned about heavenly priorities than earthly ones. For example, sometimes when women want to look beautiful, they go to great extremes—new clothes, just the right jewelry, perhaps a new hairstyle, a facial treatment, false eyelashes and fingernails, and any number of other beauty secrets. How should a Christian woman make herself beautiful? (3:1-6)

Likewise, Christian men should stand out from non-Christian men. Everyone is familiar with "locker room talk." Many guys seem to feel that it's necessary to tell sexually suggestive jokes, boast about sexual exploits, and so forth. But how should Christian men, as temporary visitors to this planet, treat the women in their lives? (3:7)

What are some other basic guidelines we should follow? (3:8-12)

As we become committed to a godly lifestyle, what are some benefits we will enjoy that others won't? (3:13-14)

Playing By Different Rules
Read 1 Peter 3:15-22.
If you are successfully setting yourself apart from the rest of the world in a positive, nonthreatening way, people are going to come up to you and say, "Hey, what gives? You're different, and I want to know why!" What should you do at that point, and what attitude should you have? (3:15-16)

Peter explained that everyone is going to suffer a bit as they go through life. People who fill their lives with alcohol, drugs, casual sex, and so forth are going to experience suffering that results from those habits. And God's people are going to go through suffering at the hands of sinful people from time to time. So since suffering can't be avoided, isn't it better to suffer for God, who will reward His heavenly minded people someday? Peter then recalled the story of Noah who "suffered" through building an ark and floating his way through the great Flood with his family and all the animals. It probably wasn't the most pleasant experience of his life, but you'd have to agree that it was preferable to the alternative (3:17-22).

Read 1 Peter 4:1-19.
In fact, we achieve a spiritual victory when we choose to suffer for our Christian beliefs. What does willful suffering indicate about a person? (4:1-2)

Many times when non-Christians see that Christians choose not to join them in their party lifestyle (drinking, sex, and other wild living), they think we're pretty strange. And perhaps if we're truthful, we sometimes feel left out. What should we remember at such times? (4:3-6)

Getting Personal — *When was the last time you experienced any suffering for your faith?*

Rather than joining in with the self-destructive lifestyle of non-Christians, we should always keep in mind that "the end of all things is near" (4:7). Consequently, what activities should we be involved in that most other people will avoid? (4:7-11)

Like James, Peter also tells us to rejoice when we suffer for our Christian faith. What reasons did Peter give for rejoicing? (4:12-18)

As we suffer—even injustly—because of our commitment to God, what should we continue to do? (4:19)

Read 1 Peter 5:1-14.
As you have seen, Christians are supposed to follow a different set of rules than the world in which they are living. And as you might expect, we are

also subject to some problems that the rest of the world will never have. If our prime concern is to lead Christian lives, and if we pour all our efforts into accomplishing that goal, have we done everything that God expects of us? Not necessarily, according to Peter. Again, our attitudes are even more important than our actions. What improper motives might we have as we claim to serve Jesus? (5:1-4)

Getting Personal — *What leadership responsibilities do you have? Do you need to reevaluate your motives for leading?*

What attitude should we have at all times? (5:5)

Why is it so important to maintain that attitude? (5:6)

Naturally, we can expect to encounter periods of worry and anxiety. What are we to do during those times? (5:7)

Peter repeatedly stressed the importance of being self-controlled (1:13; 4:7; 5:8). Why is self-control so important? (5:8)

As we determine to live for Jesus—no matter what, in all circumstances, what can we expect from God? (5:9-11)

What two people assisted Peter in his ministry? (5:12-14)

(NOTE: Peter's reference to his "son" was to indicate a spiritual closeness, not a physical relationship.)

By now, you may be thinking that Peter has asked some pretty hard things of us. You're right. It's not easy to live as a stranger on earth, to suffer, or to eliminate all worldly influences from our lives without coming across as condescending to people who notice us. Perhaps you're even asking, "Can this be the same Peter who was so wishy-washy as a disciple? Who was bold enough to walk on water one minute and insecure enough to sink the next? Who denied Jesus three times immediately after vowing to die for Him?" Yes, this is the same person. But remember that Peter had experienced the coming of the Holy Spirit on the Day of Pentecost. He had been forgiven by a resurrected Christ and was ready to live his life for Jesus only.

Peter knew what it was like to be partially committed to Jesus as well as totally committed. Having lived both ways, he could clue us into the better alternative of the two.

 JOURNEY INWARD

All we need to do is respond to what Peter has to say. And while the qualities of commitment and self-control will never come easily or automatically, we can discipline ourselves to acquire them. But to begin with, we need to develop a **future mind-set.**

If we train ourselves to constantly think of the future—beyond the daily grind of earthly life—our perspective begins to change. Try the following exercise to see if it works for you. For each situation listed, first tell how you would respond if the present were all that mattered. Then, in the last column, tell how you would respond if you were consciously thinking that your time on earth is temporary and you'll eventually be going to your real home in heaven.

Situation	Response If Your Focus Is Only On The Present	Response If Your Focus Is On The Future As Well
Your children are hassling you a lot		
You begin to date a non-Christian you really like		
Your house burns down and all you own is lost		
You would like to tell a close friend about Jesus, but you're a little scared to bring up the topic		
A close family member dies		
You're offered a job where you can make lots of money, but where the company has some shady business practices		
Your coworkers begin to make fun of your Christian beliefs		
After hearing a speaker describe a need for missionaries, you feel a strange urge to respond		
The thing you want more than anything in the world doesn't come to pass		

You'll probably notice that being future-minded won't keep you from feeling pain and grief when things go wrong. Yet it will allow you to step back from your confusion and see everything in perspective. If your focus is only on the present, then pain and grief can threaten to overcome you. But when you start to realize that your stay on earth is only temporary and that you are guaranteed a better future (a perfect one, in fact), your suffering isn't likely to be as intense.

You should also discover that a future mind-set will make your good times even better. As you look forward to eventually reaching your real home, every good event on earth can become a reminder that you have even more wonderful things to look forward to.

Challenge yourself this week to start to develop a future mind-set. Begin by setting certain times to focus on the future. After you've mastered a few short periods of time, gradually lengthen them until you regularly consider the future during all your present activities. Your life will take a big upswing as soon as you realize that your future is definitely going to be better than your present. You'll soon discover that you always have something to look forward to—when you set your mind to it.

 KEY VERSE

"Dear friends, I urge you, as aliens and strangers in the world, to abstain from sinful desires, which war against your soul. Live such good lives among the pagans that, though they accuse you of doing wrong, they may see your good deeds and glorify God on the day He visits us" (1 Peter 2:11-12).

Thousands of uninformed people are duped
into following false leaders every year.

6

WOLVES IN
SHEPHERDS' CLOTHING

(Book of 2 Peter)

H ere's a quiz for you to take to see if you're mentally ready to dive into this session. In each of the lists below, mark the item that you think doesn't belong. The answers to this exercise are at the end of the session. Check them when you're finished with all the questions to see how you did.

1.____ (A) Tallahassee
____ (B) Anchorage
____ (C) Nashville
____ (D) Sante Fe
____ (E) Frankfort

2. ____ (A) Revolver
____ (B) Help!
____ (C) Yellow Submarine
____ (D) Magical Mystery Tour
____ (E) Rubber Soul

3.____ (A) The Prince and the Pauper
____ (B) Oliver Twist
____ (C) A Christmas Carol
____ (D) Great Expectations
____ (E) David Copperfield

4. ____ (A) Baltic Avenue
____ (B) Park Place
____ (C) Reading Railroad
____ (D) Water Works
____ (E) Main Street

5.____ (A) Zeus
____ (B) Hera
____ (C) Aphrodite
____ (D) Athena
____ (E) Gus

6. ____ (A) 1
____ (B) 5
____ (C) 9
____ (D) 16
____ (E) 64

7.___ (A) Dinosaur
___ (B) Duckbilled platypus
___ (C) Passenger pigeon
___ (D) Dodo bird
___ (E) Mastadon

8. ___ (A) Calling birds
___ (B) Lords leaping
___ (C) Maids milking
___ (D) Swans swimming
___ (E) Toilets flushing

9.___ (A) Michael
___ (B) Ulysses
___ (C) Millard
___ (D) Zachary
___ (E) Grover

10. ___ (A) Otto
___ (B) Bob
___ (C) Cyril
___ (D) Hannah
___ (E) Lil

Perhaps you came up with some different answers that you felt were just as accurate as the ones given. For example, you could have selected E for question 1 because it is the only city not ending in a vowel. Or you might have come up with a correct answer, but for different reasons. Your response to question 9 might have correctly been A, but your reasoning might have been that it was the only name listed that you wouldn't be embarrassed to give to your kid.

 JOURNEY ONWARD

As we move into the Book of 2 Peter, we're going to continue the process of discovering "which one doesn't belong here." But in this case, it's not a game. Peter described a very serious problem: imposters who had infiltrated the leadership of the early church. And as you read through his first-century observations, you'll see that he could just as easily be describing today's church. The warning he sent out to his readers applies to us as well.

Peter's purpose in writing is twofold. First, he naturally wanted to warn godly people in the church to keep an eye open for leaders who might not be producing spiritual fruit. And second, Peter wanted to address the fate of the spiritual imposters themselves. So as you go through this session, try to find warning signs of deceit to look for in spiritual leaders. Also try to identify any negative characteristics of your own that you need to get rid of.

Read 2 Peter 1:1-9.
Do you think Peter's intended audience was Christians, or the people who were trying to cleverly deceive Christians? (2 Peter 1:1)

Peter knew the antidote to spiritual deceit. It is the same thing that can provide us with an abundance of grace and peace. What is it? (1:2)

With what else does this knowledge provide us? (1:3)

How is it possible to escape corruption in the world? (1:4)

Peter described a kind of spiritual chain that begins with faith and eventually produces love. While it is true that love is among the fruit of the Holy Spirit (Galatians 5:22), you don't instantly become a completely loving person the moment you become a Christian. You begin with your faith and gradually develop the kind of love that God wants you to show to others. Fill in the links of the following chain to show how Peter tells us to get from faith to love (2 Peter 1:5-7).

Getting Personal — *Where would you classify yourself on the above chain?*

As you begin to develop all these qualities, how do you know when you have enough? (1:8)

What is the alternative if you don't bother trying to develop these traits? (1:9)

A Winning Ticket
Read 2 Peter 1:10-21.
Peter then challenged us to "make [our] calling and election sure" (1:10). This is a reminder that God has "elected" (chosen) us and has called us to a

77

better way of life. We know this to be true, but from time to time we can lose track of that truth. Yet as we put into practice the qualities that Peter has been describing (the ones on our "chain"), we will be continually reminded of our special status with God. It is only through God's love and help that we can develop goodness, self-control, and so forth. What are the results of putting these characteristics into practice? (1:10-11)

Peter realized that he wasn't telling his readers any shocking new truths. What did he think about reminding them of these things they already knew? Why? (1:12-15)

Why was Peter so sure about the things he was saying about Jesus? (1:16-18; if you don't remember what Peter is talking about here, also see Matthew 17:1-8.)

What else made Peter confident that Jesus deserves our worship? (2 Peter 1:19)

What makes Bible prophecy so special? (1:20-21)

Read 2 Peter 2:1-10.
Even though God is trying to deal honestly with all of us, why are we sometimes misled about what He expects of us? (2:1-2)

What motivates such people? (2:3)

What will eventually happen to those who mislead God's people? (2:1, 3)

Getting Personal — *Have you ever been intentionally misled by a dishonest individual? What happened?*

To back up what he was saying, Peter recalled several previous examples of God's judgment. The first was God's imprisonment of disobedient angels. Then Peter named two other times when God had punished evil people while sparing the righteous ones. What two illustrations did Peter mention, and whom did God safely deliver in each case? (2:4-8)

Some people don't like to talk or think about God's judgment on evil people. But what comforting truth was Peter leading up to? (2:9-10)

Foolers and Foolees

Remember that these are supposedly religious leaders that Peter was writing about (2:1). Common sense tells us that many of the people we know will never have our best interests in mind. But we do expect pastors, Sunday School teachers, and other church leaders to be trustworthy. People posing as God's representatives for their own benefit may fool some of the people some of the time. Perhaps they can mislead some of the people all of the time, or all of the people some of the time. But God is never fooled — none of the time.

Read 2 Peter 2:10-22.

Peter didn't want us to misunderstand the concept here. Everybody is guilty of occasionally slipping behind in spiritual growth and perhaps even misinforming other people (unintentionally) about the truths of Christianity. We should try to avoid such instances, of course, but God isn't waiting around for us to make an innocent mistake so He can instantly zap us with His judgment. The people Peter referred to are those who mislead people on purpose — usually for profit. In fact, Peter provided a detailed description of such phony religious leaders. What characteristics did such people demonstrate? List all you can find in 2:10-14.

Peter compared the mentality of these people to that of an Old Testament character — Balaam. Perhaps you remember the story from Numbers 22. An enemy king paid the Prophet Balaam to curse the Israelites. God told Balaam not to do it because the Israelites were blessed. But the king raised his offer and Balaam started off. As it turned out, Balaam had a lot of transportation problems that day. He just couldn't get his donkey to go. It seems that the donkey was seeing an angel of God that Balaam couldn't see. And when Balaam started to beat the animal for the third time, the donkey turned her head around and began to have a conversation with Balaam (Numbers 22:28-31). Why do you think Peter recalled this story at this point in his writing? (2 Peter 2:15-16)

Another comparison Peter used to describe these false teachers was a dry spring (2:17). People look to their spiritual leaders for wisdom in much the same way that thirsty people approach a spring looking for refreshing water. The phony leaders could offer no solution for the spiritual thirst of the people. But even though spiritual phonies think they are successfully fooling others, Peter warned that they are the ones who don't clearly see the end results of their shameful actions. Did Peter seem to think that these people would see the error of their ways and repent? Explain your answer (2:17-22).

Coming Attractions
Read 2 Peter 3:1-14.
After the negative picture Peter had painted in regard to the false religious leaders, he changed his tone a bit. He was firm as he described the future in store for such people. But as he turned his attention to the future of God's

people, he began to warm up a bit. He reminded everyone of the real purpose of his letters. What purpose did Peter have in mind? (3:1-2)

Peter wasn't a bit surprised that he was seeing people who scoffed at the truth that Jesus had taught. Even though Jesus hadn't been gone for very long, there were already plenty of people who were trying to distort the things He had said. In this case, what predicted event were the imposters using to try to prove that Jesus wasn't keeping His promise? (3:3-4)

Peter saw right through the corrupt intentions of these people. While they were trying to convince everyone that the world seemed to be running on "automatic pilot," Peter assured his readers that this perception was false. He reminded them that God had originally created the world, largely of water. And when it came time for God's judgment of sinful people, He used water to eliminate them. The day before the big Flood, evil men were probably looking out their windows and saying, "Everything goes on as it has since the beginning of creation." There were people saying the same thing in Peter's day (3:4), and they still do today. But what assurance did Peter have for God's people? (3:5-7)

Our concept of time is a lot different than God's. We hate to wait for anything. And occasionally you hear someone say, "I waited a lifetime for this or that to happen." Well, the longest lifetime on record was Methuselah's—969 years (Genesis 5:27). In God's perception of time, about how long was the life span of Methuselah? (2 Peter 3:8)

Getting Personal—*Who is the oldest person you have ever known?*

Sometimes (especially when we've been trying very hard to live good lives), we see rotten people appearing to prosper while we continue to struggle and suffer. At such times we tend to ask why God doesn't do something to make things fair. How did Peter respond to this thought? (3:9)

Peter didn't stop there. Yes, God is patient and good. But He is also just and fair. The day will come when He finally declares that it is time to reward good and destroy evil. What will happen at that time? (3:10)

With this in mind, what should we be doing now? (3:11-12)

Why shouldn't Christians be alarmed about the eventual destruction of the heavens and the earth? (3:12-13)

Peter, knowing that many of the church members would be tempted to follow the phony leaders, left his readers with a challenge that still applies to us as members of God's church. Since they should have been eagerly anticipating the return of Jesus, what did Peter exhort them (and us) to do? (3:14)

Reading Peter to Praise Paul
Read 2 Peter 3:15-18.
We know from some of Paul's letters that he and Peter had previously had some conflict. Paul had even opposed Peter to his face—in public! (Galatians 2:11-14) Now that Peter was writing a letter of his own, he had a perfect opportunity to record just what he thought about Paul. And that's exactly what he did. What did Peter want everyone to know about Paul? (2 Peter 3:15)

Peter continued to discuss his opinions of Paul. He knew that Paul had been consistent throughout his many letters. He acknowledged that some of what Paul wrote was complex and needed serious thought to be understood. Peter wasn't protesting the fact that Paul dealt with weighty issues. (More of us need to struggle with understanding deep truths of God.) But Peter did get annoyed with some of the people who were familiar with Paul's writings. What were these people doing to draw Peter's criticism? (3:16)

In closing, Peter left his readers with a challenge of something not to do, and another challenge of something they should do. What were the two challenges with which Peter closed his second letter? (3:17-18)

 JOURNEY INWARD

In Peter's first book, he told us to watch out for outside influences (suffering, non-Christians who ridicule us, etc.) that tend to interfere with our spiritual development. In this second book, his emphasis is more on spiritual threats from inside the church. Some "religious" leaders are not sincere in their motives. Many are very clever in covering up the less-than-genuine elements of their ministries. You may wonder, "So what's the big deal if the world is full of self-seeking religious imposters? We can just avoid them, right?" Perhaps. Maybe you can avoid them. But thousands of less-informed people are duped into following these false leaders every year. So consider for a few moments the serious impact of **spiritual phonies and cults.**

Perhaps the threat of false religious leaders isn't nearly as real to you as it was to the people Peter wrote to. If you're involved in a church, you probably trust your pastor, teachers, and other leaders. In most cases, you should. Peter didn't advocate mistrusting everyone in a position of spiritual authority. But on the other hand, he didn't suggest that we close our eyes and ears to teachings that seem a little off-center either.

It may be more important than you think to work harder at understanding spiritual truths and doctrines. Everyone has an inner craving to discover spiritual truth. But many people out there are distorting the truth. They don't come right out and say, "Pssssst. Hey, buddy. Over here. I've got some new truth for you." Rather, they look and act like any other religious figure, base all their doctrines on the Bible, and distort God's truth—ever so slightly at first, and more as they begin to get your attention. And some of these guys can fool even you—unless you have a solid understanding of true biblical teaching.

Perhaps you know someone who is getting involved in a questionable religious group. Maybe you see preachers on TV who seem to be saying all the right words, yet somehow don't seem entirely trustworthy. Maybe clean-cut members of some different "brand" of religion come to your door and want to talk to you. Or perhaps you are confronted in an airport, parking lot, or some other public place. Some encounters are subtle and personal. Others are bold and challenging. So how can you tell when these guys are telling the truth—if ever? How can you help keep your friends and family from being taken in by the spiritual nonsense of these outwardly loving groups? List any people or groups whom you suspect aren't completely trustworthy below. If nobody comes to mind right away, go over the following information anyway, and try to bring it to mind when you need it.

People who have closely studied the activities of cults and similar "religious" groups notice a number of similarities to watch out for. (Many are the same things Peter told us to guard against.) The characteristics are listed below. Go down the column and check any that apply to the person or group you just listed.

❑ An attraction to "new" or "secret" truths
❑ Authority other than the Bible or new interpretation of biblical sections
❑ False methods to achieve salvation (usually by hard work)
❑ Unclear teachings and doctrines
❑ A distorted view of Jesus and/or God the Father
❑ Human leaders who have almost godlike control
❑ Monetary exploitation of followers
❑ Combining different religions to have "something for everybody"
❑ False prophecy

If you're ever attracted to certain religious groups that you don't know too much about, by all means get some solid information before you commit yourself to the group. Test everything they say they believe against the truth of the Bible. And then make sure they aren't just saying what you want to hear. They should be living it as well.

Spiritual deception is not a small problem. Peter warned about it. Paul's letters contain similar warnings. And you'll see in the next session that John backs up everything Peter and Paul said. We should avoid anyone who tries to entrap people with enticing, yet deadly, lies.

As Christians, we should also be careful not to lie to others. Sometimes we become so zealous for others to believe in Jesus that we make bold statements. "Jesus can take away all your problems." "Christians have more fun at church than non-Christians have at drinking parties." Such statements may be true for solid, mature Christians. But these promises tend to mislead people who are new to Christianity. Christians need to let others know that their religion requires a certain degree of sacrifice and discipline. As we are open and honest with others, the Holy Spirit can draw them to Christianity and away from the hundreds of other groups that would like to enslave them.

 KEY VERSE

"You must understand that no prophecy of Scripture came about by the prophet's own interpretation. For prophecy never had its origin in the will of man, but men spoke from God as they were carried along by the Holy Spirit" (2 Peter 1:20-21).

ANSWERS TO OPENING QUIZ
1. All are state capitals except (B).
2. All are Beatles album titles except (C).
3. All are Charles Dickens stories except (A).
4. All are Monopoly properties except (E).
5. All are figures in Greek mythology except (E).
6. All are squared numbers (1x1, 2x2, etc.) except (B).
7. All are extinct animals except (B).
8. All are "12 Days of Christmas" gifts except (E).
9. All are first names of U.S. Presidents except (A).
10. All are names spelled the same forward and backward except (C).

*Too often, "growing up" means growing out
of the wholesome characteristics of childlikeness.*

7

GOOD THINGS IN
YOUNG PACKAGES

(1 John, 2 John, 3 John, Jude)

Eddie and Billy are first-graders and best friends. They do everything together. Their parents have never seen two youngsters get along better. In fact, Billy and Eddie are out on the playground right now. Let's go closer and see if we can hear what they are saying. Maybe we can discover a few secrets about friendships.

"You make me sick!"

"Hah! You were born sick, you wimp."

"Who are you calling a wimp, you wimp? You can't even get all the way across the monkey bars without help."

"I hate your guts. You're so stupid."

"Stupid? If your brain were expanded to a million times its original size, it would still rattle around inside your head like a BB in a boxcar."

Oops. Perhaps we've made a mistake. Let's check and see . . . no, that's Eddie and Billy all right. But what's wrong here? Maybe we should listen again.

"I'm sorry, Billy. It was my fault."

"No way, Jose. I was wrong."

"Forget it. So whaddaya wanna do now?"

"Well, I just saw Bridgette go down to the creek. You want to go splash her?"

"Sure! Let's go."

Something about little kids makes them special. They have a marvelous way of coping with the big world that engulfs them. One minute they can be scream-ing because somebody else got a bigger piece of cake (by at least two whole crumbs), and the next minute they're giving away their favorite winter coat because they befriended a classmate at school who needed a jacket. Jesus twice singled out small children as models for Christians to imitate (Matthew 18:1-6; 19:13-14). We should try to develop a childlike degree of innocence, forgive-ness, trust in our Heavenly Father, openness, honesty, lack of prejudice, and so forth. Too often, "growing up" actually means growing out of such wholesome characteristics.

 JOURNEY ONWARD

In this session you will examine the letters of John and Jude. You will see that John repeatedly called his readers "children" or "little children." One likely reason is that he was probably old when he wrote these letters, so most of his readers would be younger than he. But we should also remember that John had been present those times that Jesus had used little children as models of proper behavior. Perhaps as John was writing, he recalled Jesus' challenge to be more childlike. As you go through this session, try to read with a childlike heart.

The writer of 1 John, 2 John, and 3 John is most likely the same John who wrote the Gospel of John and the Book of Revelation. He had been very close to Jesus, and was one of the three apostles that Jesus took with Him for special spiritual events (such as the Transfiguration [Luke 9:28-36] and prayer in the Garden of Gethsemane [Mark 14:31-32]). In these three short books, his message is one of encouragement.

1 John
Read 1 John 1:1-10.
Why did John feel qualified to tell other people about Jesus? (1 John 1:2-4)

Since John had seen, heard, and touched the living Jesus while He was on earth, John felt like he understood the message Jesus had come to tell us. What was the essence of that message? (1:5)

Getting Personal — *Are you walking in the light? When was the last time you were in spiritual darkness?*

Even though there is never any variation in God's character, we aren't always so steady. When we profess to be God's people but continue to lead sinful lives, others see us as liars. But when we are responsive to what God wants us to do, what is the result? (1:6-7)

As we develop a relationship with God, it's not long before we become aware of our sinful nature — the main factor that separates us from Him. And when we take note of our sin(s), we have two options. What are they, and what is the result of each one?

❏ OPTION #1 (1:8, 10)

❏ OPTION #2 (1:9)

Read 1 John 2:1-29.
At this point John began to address his readers as "children" (2:1). He wanted to challenge us to keep from sinning. But he knew it was unlikely that we would avoid every kind of evil. So what did he want us to know if we slipped up and did something wrong? (2:1-2)

If people claim to be Christians, what is it important for them to do? (2:3-6)

John admitted that he was not telling his readers anything new. Commandments to love one another and obey God had existed for many years (2:7). Yet in another sense, you could say that displaying love and obedience becomes new to each person who discovers the importance of these characteristics for the first time (2:8).

How does a person's relationship with God translate into relationships with fellow Christians? (2:9-11)

John was firm in regard to those who were inconsistent in their spiritual behavior. But he knew that many people were remaining strong in their faith. So he paused to assure them that he knew they were, for the most part, being faithful (2:12-14). What things did John say were likely to stand in the way of faithfulness? (2:15-16)

What's one of the major differences between living for God and living to please yourself? (2:17)

Getting Personal — *Are your desires always different from God's desires for you?*

What did John call people who claimed to serve Jesus but really worked against Him? (2:18-19)

What is perhaps the world's biggest lie? (2:20-23)

Little children need to be reminded often of what is right and wrong—even though they know. John didn't hesitate to remind his "children" of what they already knew either. He gently prodded his readers to "see that what you have heard from the beginning remains in you" (2:24). What good reason did John give for faithfully continuing in our faith? (2:25-29)

Read 1 John 3:1-24.
John isn't the only one who thought of believers as "children"—so does God (3:1). And as children of God, what is one thing we can look forward to? (3:1-3)

Is it possible to get any indication as to which people are children of God? Explain (3:4-10).

John referred to Cain, whose lack of love led to murder. Then John gave us the standard of true love. What is it? (3:11-16)

While this example is a little extreme, love almost always requires sacrifice. What other kinds of sacrificial actions prove our love for others? (3:17-20)

⟨

Getting Personal—*What person taught you what real love is all about?*

But sacrificial love has certain rewards. What are some of them? (3:21-24)

Read 1 John 4:1-21.
As John reminded God's people to be loving and obedient, he also issued a warning. We're not supposed to be naive or stupid. We should know to whom we give our love and to whom we are being obedient. Not everyone can be trusted. So how can we determine whether to be nice or to avoid someone? (4:1-3)

What reassuring fact did John insert at this point? (4:4-6)

What is the connection between God and love? List all the tie-ins you can find in 4:7-16.

What is the connection between fear and love? (4:17-18)

Getting Personal—*Have you ever been afraid to express love to another person? How could love help you get rid of that fear?*

How can we tell when someone doesn't really love God but is just saying that he does? (4:19-21)

Read 1 John 5:1-21.
OK, children, one more time. Read 1 John 5:1-5 and see how John again summarized what he had been saying. But don't take his summaries lightly.

They are eternal truths that need to be drilled into our hearts and minds until they come out through our behavior.

At this point, John began to talk about Jesus, water, and blood. His comments may sound a little strange until you put them into context. Some of the misguided religious leaders in John's day were called Gnostics. Their religion, Gnosticism, taught that Jesus was born as a man and became the Son of God at His baptism. Then He supposedly became human again sometime before His crucifixion. John made it clear that Jesus "did not come by water only, but by water and blood" (5:6). In other words, Jesus was just as much God at His crucifixion as at His baptism. Otherwise, He would have been just a regular guy who died for the sins of the world, which wouldn't do much for our standing with God! (Do you see how false religious teachers start with some degree of truth and twist it a little at a time until it's not true at all?)

As hard as it is to understand, the truth of the Gospel is that Jesus was both God and man—at His birth, at His baptism, and at His crucifixion. If you need more proof, John suggests that you consider the presence of the Holy Spirit in your life. The same Holy Spirit that descended at Jesus' baptism to confirm that He is the Son of God (Matthew 3:16-17) lives within Christians today to testify to the same fact. So John says to consider Jesus' baptism ("the water"), His crucifixion ("the blood"), and the presence of the Holy Spirit. When people consider these things and come to the conclusion that Jesus is indeed the Son of God and worthy of their worship, what is in store for them? (1 John 5:6-12)

As children of God anticipating eternal life with Him, what special privileges do we have? (5:13-15)

When we observe a fellow child of God commit a sin, what is our responsibility? (5:16-17)

It's hard to tell exactly what John meant when he referred to "a sin that leads to death" (5:16). The Bible is clear in stating that all sin leads to death eventually—if we don't receive Jesus' forgiveness for our sin (Romans 6:23). But John seems to be referring to a specific kind of sin in this passage. Perhaps he had in mind a sin that could lead to physical death (as Paul had referred to in 1 Corinthians 11:29-30). Another possibility is that John was talking about the Gnostics, whose stubborn refusal to accept the simple truth of the Gospel would ultimately result in spiritual death. But regardless of any uncertainty we may have regarding the specific interpretation, it's clear that sin—any sin—is serious. Whenever we discover it in our own lives, we need to eliminate it right away. And if we see it in the life of someone we care about, we need to spend some serious time in prayer for that person.

As John closed his first letter, he listed three things we can be sure of. What are the three things that "we know"? (1 John 5:18-21)

2 John
Read 2 John 1-13.
John's second letter, written at about the same time as the first, was addressed to "the chosen lady and her children" (2 John 1). We don't know if this was an actual family, or symbolic of a church and its members. But either way, he wrote to address a specific problem. Christian preachers at this time often traveled around, and were usually fed, housed, and otherwise supported by good-hearted Christian people. The trouble was that Gnostic teachers also began to travel, and some good Christians were unwittingly supporting this false teaching by providing the Gnostics with all they needed. What did John want the well-meaning Christians to know and to do? (2 John 1-13)

3 John
Read 3 John 1-14.
John's third letter, also written at about the same time, was a little more personal. It was written to "my dear friend Gaius" (3 John 1). Gaius was being faithful to his Christian beliefs. But another person, Diotrephes, was a church leader who wasn't being so faithful. What was the problem with Diotrephes, and what advice did John give? (3 John 1-14)

Getting Personal — *When it comes to hospitality, are you more like Gaius or Diotrephes?*

Jude

Read Jude 1-25.

While you're skimming through all these short New Testament books, go on to the next one—the Book of Jude. The name *Jude* is a form of Judah or Judas. The author of this book might have been one of Jesus' disciples, though it doesn't seem likely because he doesn't seem to associate himself with the apostles. (In addition to Judas Iscariot, Jesus had another disciple named Judas. See Luke 6:16.) Most likely, this Jude was perhaps a brother of Jesus (Matthew 13:55).

Jude wanted to write about the joys of our salvation, but he didn't. Why not? (Jude 1-4)

As Peter had done, Jude listed some examples to show that he was aware that God rewarded good and judged evil. In the last session, you saw Peter's examples: disobedient angels, Noah, Sodom and Gomorrah, and Lot (2 Peter 2:4-8). What example did Jude add? (Jude 5-7)

One of the interesting things about Jude's short book is that he makes references to what is called apocryphal material. (This is information of a religious nature that the authorities didn't feel was quite authentic enough to include in the "official" Scriptures.) The fact that Jude used such material doesn't necessarily mean he believed it. It would be like your referring to Zeus, Thor, or Paul Bunyan in a term paper. It doesn't mean you believe they really existed, but it shows you're aware of the stories and can use them to make a point. Jude wanted to make the point that we shouldn't be hasty to criticize God or His heavenly creations; so what apocryphal story did he refer to? (Jude 8-10)

Jude also referred to several Old Testament stories: Cain (Genesis 4), Balaam (Numbers 22), and Korah (Numbers 16). All were examples of misguided, disobedient men who stubbornly followed their own instincts instead of God's guidance. Jude likened such men to the false religious leaders of his time. How did Jude describe these religious leaders? (Jude 11-16; note the quotation in verses 14-15 from another apocryphal source, the Book of Enoch.)

What advice did Jude offer concerning the false religious leaders? (17-25)

So Jude agreed with John who agreed with Peter who agreed with Paul who agreed with any number of faithful people of God. And what they all agreed on is that phony religious leaders should be avoided. So now we need to figure out how we can be smart enough to avoid clever and tricky people while we act like "little children."

 JOURNEY INWARD

First we need to decide exactly what is so special about children. You see, even though Jesus expressed His desire for us to be more like little children, the Apostle Paul wrote about the importance of putting "childish ways behind me" (1 Corinthians 13:11). And yet it is inconceivable that Paul and Jesus would disagree on a major point or that either one would be in error concerning spiritual truth; so let's assume they were both right. If so, we might agree with Paul's desire to eliminate childish behavior. But at the same time, we can respond to Jesus' challenge to develop a characteristic that is rare these days — **childlikeness.**

So what's the difference between childishness and childlikeness? According to the dictionary, *childish* means "marked by immaturity and lack of poise." *Childlike* is the opposite: "marked by innocence, trust, and ingenuousness." If you watch small children closely, you see both extremes. In the first column below, list all the the qualities you can think of that you consider childish. In the second column, list everything you would consider childlike. In each case, a couple are provided to get you started.

CHILDISH QUALITIES	CHILDLIKE QUALITIES
Immaturity	Innocence
Clumsiness	Trust
Selfishness	Friendliness

The trouble with childish habits is that it's often hard to outgrow them. And the problem with childlike characteristics is that they are hard to retain. But just because these things are hard to do doesn't mean we shouldn't be trying to do them.

Go through both of the lists. Circle any of the words that accurately describe yourself. If you circle more in the **Childlike** column than the **Childish** column, good for you. You're on the right track. If you circle more in the **Childish** column, you have a little more work to do.

Anything circled in the **Childish** column is an area you need to eliminate. And anything uncircled in the **Childlike** column is a goal to work toward. The more effort you make to accomplish these things, the more you will realize that both Jesus and Paul were right. We should strive to be like little children (childlike). Yet we are to leave childish things behind us.

As John and Jude have told us, we need both perspectives. As Christians who imitate Jesus, we are supposed to be childlike. We are God's children and need to develop all the good qualities of our Father. But at the same time, a lot of false teachers out in the world would like to "adopt" us. If we are childish (greedy, self-centered, etc.), we can easily be taken in by them. But we're not to let that happen. So it's time to grow up and do the childlike thing. (And hurry up. It's almost time for recess.)

 KEY VERSE

"How great is the love the Father has lavished on us, that we should be called children of God!" (1 John 3:1)

97

*How often do we evaluate our churches based on procedures, buildings, and
traditions rather than how well individuals fulfill their roles and
work together as a group?*

8

CHECKING OUT THE CHURCHES
(Revelation 1–3)

The organ was playing softly to correspond with the "Silent Meditation" portion of the bulletin (just prior to starting the church service). So naturally, Susan's husband Ken was fidgeting.

"C'mon, Honey! If we leave right now, we can be home in time for the kickoff. It's not too late. The music's still playing."

Several church members raised their eyebrows as Ken started to gather his things. But Susan protested.

"We can watch the game after church. We should stay till the service is over."

"Why?"

Susan answered the question with one of her own. "Why shouldn't we?" She was instantly sorry she asked.

"Because it's BOR-ing! Because all we do is sit here, read our Sunday School papers, write notes, and whisper. I fall asleep during the long prayers. All the hymns are from the Dark Ages or something. The sermons have nothing to do with our lives. These people wouldn't even miss us if we weren't here."

Susan hadn't been able to get a word in edgewise. Finally she whispered a little too harshly—"Shut up!" The elderly couple in front of them (both with hearing aids) turned their heads, pointed their eyes toward Susan and Ken, and gave them a miniglare. Lowering her voice, Susan protested a little more quietly, "Some of what you say is true, but church is still important for us."

"OK," challenged Ken. "You've heard my reasons. So tell me why you think we should go to church. Give me your Top Ten reasons to attend church."

Susan got that sinking feeling in the pit of her stomach, but she bravely pressed on. "OK. Let's see. We should go to church to help support the other people here."

"That's one."

"We should get in the habit of going while we're still young."

"That's two."

"It helps us grow spiritually."

"That's questionable, but I'll count it as number three."

"We should go because . . . it's important to. . . ."

But at that exact moment the Pastor stepped to the pulpit to begin the Call to Worship. Susan had stalled long enough to stay today, but she was concerned about the weeks to come. She knew deep down inside that her husband's reasons to skip church sounded more convincing than her reasons to attend. And she began to wonder if maybe he could be right.

•••

It's a common practice to evaluate (criticize?) church procedures and traditions. The problem is, we are being hard on ourselves when we do so. Throughout the New Testament it is very clear that the church is not a specific building, but rather a collection of Christian people with individual and specific gifts. The success or failure of the church depends on how well that bunch of people fulfill their individual roles and work together as a group.

To sit in the back, contributing nothing and complaining about everyone else is like a football player who fumbles the ball, walks to the sidelines, and yells,

"You guys really stink!" You can't disassociate yourself from the rest of the group. If you have problems with your church, it's a problem with yourself.

When church congregations fall short of what they are supposed to be, it may be hard to correct the problem from within. Voices get raised, feelings get hurt, and hearts become hardened toward each other and toward God. In extreme cases, it may be best to bring in an outside consultant to evaluate the church—someone who is both experienced and impartial. In lieu of that, the members of the church just have to work out their problems the best way they can.

 JOURNEY ONWARD

In this session, however, you will read about seven churches who found themselves in the unusual situation of being evaluated by a completely fair and knowledgeable outside party—Jesus Himself. In this and the next four sessions, we will be working our way through the Book of Revelation. No doubt you've heard a lot about Revelation—the Antichrist, the number 666, plagues, the four horsemen of the Apocalypse, and so forth. But hold your horsemen, because this session will be pretty tame compared with the ones that follow.

Read Revelation 1:1-20.
If you were paying attention in the last session, you may recall that the Apostle John was the one to whom God gave the responsibility for writing Revelation. How did John know what to write, and what is the purpose of his writing? (Revelation 1:1-2)

The Book of Revelation is sometimes confusing and has led to a number of conflicting opinions among good people. Why shouldn't we just skip it altogether? (1:3)

John addressed his writing to "the seven churches in the province of Asia" (1:4). These churches will be identified and described in chapters 2 and 3. They were located in the province of Asia Minor, in an approximate circle within 50 miles of each other. John sent these churches greetings from Jesus. What titles did he use to describe Him? (1:4-6)

What did John say was about to happen? (1:7)

What title did John use to describe God? Why? (1:8)

John wasn't exactly sitting around in his office, looking for a new book to write. Rather, he had been arrested by the Roman government for expressing his Christian beliefs. They had sentenced him to exile on Patmos—an island in the Aegean Sea (off the coast of what is now Turkey). What happened to John on the Island of Patmos? (1:9-11)

You'll discover more about these seven churches soon. But before he started writing, John wanted to take a peek at who was talking to him. When he turned around, what did he see? (1:12-16)

How did John, the disciple who had spent so much time with Jesus, respond to this sight? (1:17)

The figure thought John could use an explanation for all these strange things he was seeing. So how did He explain:

❑ Himself? (1:17-18)

❏ The seven lampstands? (1:20)

❏ The seven stars? (1:20)

The next two chapters follow a straightforward pattern. John relayed Jesus' words to all seven of the churches. In each case, Jesus first identified the church by addressing its "angel" (pastor). Then He provided: (1) a description of Himself; (2) a notation of the good things about the church; (3) a notation of the bad things about the church; (4) a challenge (warning); and (5) a promise. In a couple of places, one of the categories was omitted (say, for instance, if a church was doing everything right). In several instances, Jesus' instructions had a direct bearing on the specific characteristics of the city in which the church was located. Read each of the following descriptions carefully, and then fill in the information for each church.

Ephesus
Read Revelation 2:1-7.
You may remember the city of Ephesus from Paul's travels in the Book of Acts. It was a large seaport noted for its commercial trade and was the most important city in Asia Minor. It also contained the large temple dedicated to the goddess Artemis. Review Revelation 2:1-7 and record:

❏ The description of Jesus—

❏ The good things about the church—

❏ The bad things about the church—

❏ Jesus' challenge—

❏ Jesus' promise—

What do you think Jesus meant when He said to the Ephesians, "You have forsaken your first love"? (2:4)

[NOTE: The Nicolaitans (2:6) were a group of people who believed that their spiritual freedom made it OK to worship idols and fool around sexually.]

Smyrna
Read Revelation 2:8-11.
A popular trend at this time was emperor-worship (treating the Roman leader as a god). Many people in Smyrna were closely tied to Rome and eager to please the Roman authorities. However, the church didn't necessarily follow the leading of the townspeople. Smyrna was large, beautiful, and wealthy, as well. Many Jewish people lived there who were hostile to Christians. Review Revelation 2:8-11 and fill in the information about this church.

❏ The description of Jesus—

❏ The good things about the church—

❏ The bad things about the church—

❏ Jesus' challenge —

❏ Jesus' promise —

If you had lived in Smyrna, do you think you would have stuck with the poverty-stricken, persecuted church? Or would you have tried to enjoy the wealth and splendor of the city? Explain.

Getting Personal — *Has it been more difficult for you to remain faithful when you've had plenty of money or when your budget was tight?*

Pergamum
Read Revelation 2:12-17.
Pergamum was another wealthy, wicked city. Its people worshiped a wide assortment of gods and goddesses. It was also the center of emperor-worship in Asia. Pergamum was noted for its university and large library, as well as its manufacture of a special parchment/paper (*pergamena*). Review Revelation 2:12-17 and record what you find.

❏ The description of Jesus —

❏ The good things about the church —

❏ The bad things about the church —

❑ Jesus' challenge—

❑ Jesus' promise—

[NOTE: Antipas is thought to have been the first Christian martyr in Asia. According to tradition, during the reign of Emperor Domitian, Antipas was placed in a bronze kettle and slowly roasted to death.]

Thyatira
Read Revelation 2:18-29.
The city of Thyatira wasn't large, but it was noted for its trade guilds, rich crops, and special purple cloth. It was also a military base. Review Revelation 2:18-29 and record what Jesus had to say about the church in this city.

❑ The description of Jesus—

❑ The good things about the church—

❑ The bad things about the church—

❑ Jesus' challenge—

❑ Jesus' promise —

[NOTE: *Jezebel* is a reference to an evil Old Testament queen (1 Kings 16:31). The name can be assigned to anyone who follows her wicked practices of idolatry and disregard for true worship to God.]

Sardis
Read Revelation 3:1-6.
Sardis was another major city — wealthy and famous, and located on a busy trade route. Jewelry, dye, and textiles were abundant. An acropolis sat high on one of the local mountains. Review Revelation 3:1-6 and record what you find.

❑ The description of Jesus —

❑ The good things about the church —

❑ The bad things about the church —

❑ Jesus' challenge —

❑ Jesus' promise —

What do you think the Book of Life is? (3:5; also see Exodus 32:31-33.)

[NOTE: Archeologists have discovered the remains of a Christian church building in Sardis—right next to the temple of Artemis.]

Getting Personal — *Do you think your name is in the Book of Life? Why or why not?*

Philadelphia
Read Revelation 3:7-13.
Your study of American history may have taught you that the word *philadelphia* means "brotherly love." This Philadelphia was located in an area prone to earthquakes. The city had already been destroyed and rebuilt several times. Review Revelation 3:7-13 and describe the church in this New Testament city of brotherly love.

❑ The description of Jesus—

❑ The good things about the church—

❑ The bad things about the church—

❑ Jesus' challenge—

❑ Jesus' promise—

Laodicea

Read Revelation 3:14-22.

Last, and perhaps least, is the church in Laodicea. The city was wealthy and known for banking, the manufacture of fine wool cloth and clothes, and a medical school famous for its eye salve. One shortcoming of the city was an insufficient supply of water. As you study Revelation 3:14-22, look for hints that Jesus was aware of the pros and cons of the city. Write down what you find.

❑ The description of Jesus—

❑ The good things about the church—

❑ The bad things about the church—

❑ Jesus' challenge—

❑ Jesus' promise—

Getting Personal—*If you took your spiritual temperature today, what would be the result?*

Some people think that the order in which Jesus addressed the churches reflects church history from first-century times until now (beginning with a drop in devotion [Ephesus], significant amounts of persecution [Smyrna, Pergamum], and working down to today's lukewarmness [Laodicea]).Whether or not this is true, these churches were actual historic places with individual strengths and shortcomings.

JOURNEY INWARD

If you were expecting multitudes of angels and awe-inspiring heavenly conflict from this first session in Revelation, you may be disappointed. After all, you found yourself in church—seven of them, to be exact. But the contrasts among the churches provide a needed background for the things that will come in the next sessions. And before you complete this session, you need to take a look at one more church—your own. So spend a little time **evaluating your church.**

The condition of your church may not seem too important to you, but it is to Jesus. You might want to use the same outline that Jesus used when addressing the seven first-century churches as you evaluate the church you attend. Try to go beyond things like, "The sermons are too long" and so forth. Rather, look at things like spiritual commitment, willingness to with stand opposition, influence in the community, etc. Record your observations in the outline that follows.

❑ Description of Jesus—If Jesus were to appear to your church congregation, which of His characteristics do you think He would emphasize? (Faithfulness? Power? Righteousness? Or what?)

❑ Good things about your church—What are the things your church is doing right that you think Jesus would comment on?

❑ Bad things about your church—What weaknesses do you think Jesus would point out? What things do you need to do better? What things are you doing that you shouldn't do?

❑ The challenge—What things do you think Jesus would challenge your congregation to do?

❑ The promise—What truth would motivate your church members to persevere in their faith no matter what?

As you went through Jesus' messages to the seven churches, did you notice His emphasis on overcoming? It's hard to face lengthy opposition and overcome it. But that's where the rewards are. We should work on overcoming the problems we face. Someday we will discover that it was worth the effort.

 KEY VERSE

"Here I am! I stand at the door and knock. If anyone hears My voice and opens the door, I will come in and eat with him, and he with Me. To him who overcomes, I will give the right to sit with Me on My throne, just as I overcame and sat down with My Father on His throne" (Revelation 3:20-21).

*Someday all creatures in heaven and on earth will
stop whatever they are doing and praise God.*

9

VIEW FROM THE TOP

(Revelation 4:1–8:5)

Oops. In the fastidious preparation of this book, we've made a little mistake. You see, this is the last book in the New Testament series, and everyone was in such a hurry to get it to press. We've checked all the Bible references and done the really important stuff, but unfortunately the proofreaders overlooked one little section. If you wouldn't mind too much, would you fix the punctuation and capitalization in the following paragraph for us? We would really appreciate it.

••

he is a young man yet experienced in the works of sin he is never found in opposing vice and wickedness he takes delight in the downfall of his neighbors he never rejoices in the prosperity of his friends he is always ready to help in destroying the peace of society he takes no pleasure in serving the Lord he is uncommonly active in spreading hatred among his friends he takes no pride in helping to promote the cause of Christianity he has not been careless in trying to tear down the church he makes no effort to overcome his evil passions he strives hard to build up Satan's kingdom he lends no aid to the support of the Gospel among heathen people he contributes largely to the devil he will never go to heaven he must go where he will receive his just reward

••

Your impression of this person will depend on your punctuation. If your first sentence was, "He is a young man, yet experienced in the works of sin," then you may not consider him a desirable role model. But the paragraph

113

could have begun, "He is a young man, yet experienced. In sin, he is never found." And so forth. In this version, the last sentence would read, "To heaven he must go, where he will receive his just reward." Try reading the paragraph both ways, and see how you come out. (By the way, this paragraph was borrowed from the *Ideas* series published by Youth Specialties.)

It's amazing how different people can sometimes look at the same group of words on a page and come up with drastically different conclusions. Perhaps you've been shown optical illusions where you see one thing and someone else sees a completely different image. Usually it is only after you talk to each other that you can discover why the other person couldn't see what was so clear to you. And often it turns out that you were both half right— and half wrong.

 JOURNEY ONWARD

So why all this talk about punctuation and optical illusions? Well, in this session you're about to go deeper into the Book of Revelation. Before you do, it's important to remember that sometimes things may not be exactly what you perceive them to be. Other people may have vastly different opinions than yours, and in many cases you may both be correct. As you approach Revelation, it is important to look for things that you can agree on rather than seeking opportunities for conflict.

Revelation is the only biblical book written in what is called *apocalyptic* language—a form of writing that is full of symbolism. Certain objects or people will often represent other things. To complicate matters more, Revelation contains many new and practically indescribable things. Even if we were seeing the events take place before our eyes, we might not be able to agree on everything we had seen. So be patient and understanding as you study this book, especially if you're in a group study.

But even though Revelation is a tough book to understand, don't be intimidated by it. Many of the facts will be clear and straightforward. Hold tightly to those clear truths as you form your own opinions about the other things that are more open to interpretation.

Back to the Future
Read Revelation 4:1-11.
We saw in the last session that John had taken a lot of dictation to send out to the seven churches. What happened to him when he completed that task? (4:1)

Put yourself in John's place. You're faithfully doing something God has told you to do, you get to a good breaking point, and God says, "Come here a minute. I want to show you something." That sensation in itself would overwhelm the strongest person. But before he could even catch his breath, John began taking in sights that perhaps no living human had ever seen before. Review Revelation 4:2-8 and describe the things that John saw.

❏ The throne

❏ The figure on the throne

❏ The 24 elders

❏ The general surroundings

❑ The four living creatures

[NOTE: *Jasper* and *Carnelian* (v. 3) are types of see-through quartz, most likely green and red, respectively. The 24 elders (v. 4) may be symbolic of the believers in God in heaven, or could be a special group of angels.]

Skim the same passage and this time note the sounds that John was hearing.

Obviously, the 24 elders were a special group. They had somehow been given the wonderful privilege of surrounding the throne of God. They had been rewarded with crowns of gold. What did they do with their well-deserved crowns? (4:9-11)

Read Revelation 5:1-14.
As John looked on, there seemed to be a problem in the heavenly scene. What happened that caused concern? (5:1-4)

How was this problem resolved? (5:5)

Jesus had been described to John as the "Lion of the tribe of Judah." But when John looked, what did he see? (5:6)

As you've probably figured out by now, the number seven symbolizes completeness. Horns were an Old Testament symbol of power. So what do you think is the significance of Jesus being seen as having seven horns and seven eyes?

When Jesus took the scroll from God the Father, how did the 24 elders and 4 living creatures respond? (5:7-10)

Who joined them in their response? (5:11-12)

Who else eventually joined in? (5:13-14)

Getting Personal — *What does this passage indicate about the power of music and praise? What was the best choir or musical group you have ever heard?*

Exactly why was Jesus qualified to open the scroll and make everyone so jubilant? (5:9)

Seven Seals
Read Revelation 6:1-17.
The scroll Jesus had been handed had seven seals on it. What happened as He opened each of the first four seals?

☐ SEAL #1 (6:1-2)

☐ SEAL #2 (6:3-4)

☐ SEAL #3 (6:5-6)

☐ SEAL #4 (6:7-8)

[NOTE: Some people think the rider of the white horse was Jesus because white horses represented victory. Others think that since Jesus appears as a conqueror at the end of the period of Tribulation, this rider must be the Antichrist. A third interpretation is that the rider represents the spirit of Conquest in general, since he rides with Bloodshed, Famine, and Death.]

Read carefully as you go through these passages. Some facts are clear: If war, famine, plague, and wild animals kill over a fourth of the earth's population (v. 8) by today's count, that would be over a billion people. Other observations are more subtle. For instance, the fact that the first rider has a bow with no mention of an arrow is interpreted by some people to mean that he will conquer by peaceful means. Don't just skim over all the details; look closely.

When the fifth seal was opened, what did John see and hear? (6:9-11)

The situation got worse as the sixth seal was opened. What chain of events takes place at this point? (6:12-17)

Getting Personal — *How does this chapter make you feel about the end times? Will your response affect your actions?*

Read Revelation 7:1-17.
A good question is raised in the previous passage: "Who can stand?" As far as people on earth could tell, the world was coming to an end. Never in history had they heard of such a severe devastation. What they didn't realize is that God was finally allowing a degree of destruction to take place that He had withheld for so long. So the correct answer to the question, "Who can stand?" is "Anyone whom God designates." God would allow a significant number of people to stand during all the surrounding turmoil. How many people are mentioned and what would be special about them? (7:1-8)

The next thing John saw was a multitude of people so numerous that no one could count them. What were these people like, and what were they doing? (7:9-12)

119

Getting Personal — *Which praise words ascribed to God in this passage seem most significant to you?*

At this point, one of the 24 elders strolled over to John and asked him who he thought these people were. John politely tossed the question back to the elder. What did the elder tell John about these people in white robes? (7:13-17)

Notice here the phrase used by the elder to describe all the terrible things that are happening: the Great Tribulation (v. 14). Notice also that God's people who died during the Tribulation were given an exceptionally rewarding function in heaven. And never again would they have to suffer.

Read Revelation 8:1-5.
At this time, the seventh and last seal was opened. What happened as soon as Jesus opened this seal? (8:1)

Seven angels were given trumpets (8:2). These trumpets would be sounded in succession much in the same way the seals were opened, though the trumpets were all part of the seventh seal. But before the trumpet judgments began to take place, another angel appeared with a golden censer (a bowl-shaped container supported by chains, like a hanging flowerpot). In the Old Testament, a copper censer was used to transfer coals from the outside altar (where animals were sacrificed) to the inside altar of incense. What was in this angel's censer? (8:3-4)

After the contents of the censer were presented to God, what happened to the censer? (8:5)

What Does It All Mean?

We'll save the seven trumpets and their effects on the world until next session. But before we move on, let's consider some definitions and some traditional interpretations of what has been going on in this session.

The Great Tribulation—This is the terrible judgment of God on sinful and unrepentant humankind. You'll read more about it as you go through the rest of Revelation. Many people believe that this event will last seven years (Daniel 9:26-27). This will be "a time of distress such as has not happened from the beginning of nations until then" (Daniel 12:1).

The Antichrist—This is the evil world ruler referred to by Daniel. In previous New Testament books you have seen mentions of "antichrists," defined as anyone opposed to the truths of Jesus. But during the Great Tribulation, a man of exceptional power and persuasion will come to rule. In the next session, you will learn more about this person.

The Rapture—Though this term is never used in the Bible, it is a common reference to the time that Christians will be called up into heaven (1 Thessalonians 4:15-18). This event is to be accompanied with "the voice of the archangel and with the trumpet call of God" (1 Thessalonians 4:16).

At this point we need to consider a couple of hard questions.

QUESTION #1—Are these people and events in Revelation to be interpreted literally, or are they primarily symbolic of good and evil? And if they are literal accounts, have they already taken place or are they yet to come? Here are several common viewpoints:

❏ *Opinion #1*—Revelation is a symbolic description of the Christian church in the first century, under the tyranny of the Roman Empire. Its theme of good vs. evil refers to Christians vs. Romans.

❏ *Opinion #2* — Revelation is symbolic of church history from the end of the first century until the end of time. The opening of each of the seals, for example, would be associated with a specific event in history that affected the church.

❏ *Opinion #3* — The events in Revelation are, for the most part, literal. Therefore, most of these things must take place in the future (since they haven't happened yet).

❏ *Opinion #4* — Revelation only symbolizes the continual struggle between good and evil, and shouldn't be tied into any specific time period.

(While each of the opinions may have certain benefits, the authors are closest to Opinion #3 — that most of the events described in Revelation are not entirely symbolic and are yet to come. But you should search the Scriptures yourself, consult your church leaders about what they believe on these matters, and come to an intelligent decision.)

QUESTION #2 — Will the Rapture take place before or after the Tribulation? In other words, will Christians have to experience the backlash of God's fury against a sinful world?

This question raises a lot of debate. Some people say yes. Definitely. Jesus returns at the end of the Tribulation to claim His faithful followers. Other people disagree. They quote verses such as 2 Peter 2:9 and Revelation 2:24-25 to justify their belief that God will spare His people from such intense conflict. They point out that the lampstands (churches) were on earth in Revelation 1:12 and in heaven in Revelation 4:5.

The individual considerations of this question are too numerous and too complex to allow detailed contrast here. You should discuss this topic (and other debatable issues) with your pastor and ask specific questions as they come to mind. But as you go through Revelation on your own, here are some guidelines to keep in mind:

❏ The *order* of the events isn't as important as the *facts* of the events. In other words, don't miss out on all these incredible last-days revelations just because you're not sure whether or not the Rapture should have already taken place.

During the Tribulation, there will be a number of people who faithfully maintain a belief in Jesus. It's not essential to know if these people were Christians before the Tribulation or if they became Christians during the Tribulation.

❑ The clear purpose of Revelation is to detail the victory of God over Satan—not to determine the victory of pretribulation rapture people over posttribulation rapture people (or vice versa).

If you haven't yet developed an opinion on this issue, fine. Just keep an open mind as you look at the facts in Revelation. If you do have an opinion, that's OK too. Just be aware that you may not be 100 percent right, and other people may not be 100 percent wrong.

As you go through the Book of Revelation, write down your questions. After you've seen everything Revelation has to say, take your list to your pastor, Sunday School teacher, or a knowledgeable person and get their opinions. Compare everything you hear or read with the biblical account to find an interpretation that makes good sense to you.

JOURNEY INWARD

Amid all of his confusion and the incredible action taking place, John did an amazing thing. How many people in John's unique position would have taken time to be concerned with the exact words and people who were offering praise to God? But look at John's repeated emphasis on **the importance of praise**: Revelation 4:8, 11; 5:9-10, 12-14; 7:10-17. John recorded the praise of the 24 elders, the 4 living creatures, the millions of angels, the creatures of heaven and earth, and the martyrs.

If praise was so important to all these people—and to John—as the world was coming apart around them, then perhaps we need to take it a lot more seriously. Sure, we know in our heads that we should praise God regularly. But do we really have a heartfelt commitment to stop whatever we're doing and offer praise to God? Below is a Praise Profile to help you evaluate your praise habits.

WHO: When you offer praise, to whom do you direct it? In this section of Revelation, some praise was given to God the Father and some to Jesus. Do you usually praise "God" in general, or do you offer specific praise to Jesus, God the Father, and the Holy Spirit?

WHAT: What reasons do you have to offer praise? Do you get stuck in a rut, mechanically praising God for the same things? Think of some previously unthought-of reasons to give praise to:

❏ God the Father

❏ Jesus

❏ The Holy Spirit

WHEN AND WHERE: Do you have regularly scheduled times to give praise to God? If not, when would be a good time? What are some of the times and places where perhaps you should have stopped to say thanks to God, but didn't?

WHY: This is the big question. Why do you offer praise to God? Is it something you do only out of habit or obligation? Or is your praise always genuine? When you sing the doxology in church, do you think about the words? When you say grace before a meal, can you overcome the smell of the turkey in order to focus on God? What things do you need to do to make your praise more sincere?

Someday all creatures in heaven and on earth will stop whatever they are doing and praise God (Revelation 5:13). But why not get an early start and begin to offer genuine praise because you want to? After all, it will be an eternal activity. If it plays such a major part in the climactic last days of earth, it surely deserves our time here and now.

 KEY VERSE

"Worthy is the Lamb, who was slain, to receive power and wealth and wisdom and strength and honor and glory and praise!" (Revelation 5:12)

The better you know your opponent,
the better you will be at defending yourself.

10

DUNGEON AND DRAGON

(Revelation 8:6–13:18)

On August 2, 1990 Iraq, led by President Saddam Hussein, invaded the country of Kuwait. On November 29, 1990 the United Nations set a deadline for Iraqi withdrawal from Kuwait. On January 16, 1991 (just one day past the UN deadline) the United States, along with allied forces, attacked Iraq in a mission to liberate Kuwait.

Picture, if you will, this imaginary scenario taking place on January 16.

The General sounded confident and professional as he explained Operation Desert Storm's plans to his officers. They had already heard the strategy many times—before every Pentagon briefing, in fact. But today they were looking to the General for something more. They needed direction in this, the biggest conflict in their lives.

"So, General," ventured one of the officers, "what do we need to do defensively? Are these guys more of a threat on the ground or in the air?"

"I can't rightly say, Son," responded the General. "We haven't had a chance to see any of the surveillance films."

Another officer asked, "What kind of fighting history do they have?"

"Don't know that, either," said the General. "I probably should have checked, but I just didn't get around to it."

The next question was a little more reserved. "Then, uh, what can you tell us about the Iraqis? Do they have a big front line? Are they quick? What can we expect to face in the desert?"

"Those are fine questions, Son, and I wish I knew the answers. But I don't. You're just going to have to go out there and do your best."

By now the whole group of officers was growing concerned. "Well, what kind of offense are we going to run?" "What kind of special forces are we up against?" "If we get an early advantage, do you want us to keep fighting all out, or scale back?"

But the General had no idea. By the time his forces hit the desert, their optimism had completely evaporated. They had no idea what to expect, so they expected the worst—that they would never succeed in their mission.

Whenever you find yourself in a conflict situation, you'll discover that the more you know about your opponent, the better you'll be able to defend yourself. How often do you fall just short of winning a game, debate, argument, or client because you don't know quite enough about your opponent?

 JOURNEY ONWARD

The same principle applies to your spiritual life. If you know the strategies of your enemy, Satan, you won't be so likely to fall into temptation. As we move forward into the next section of Revelation, you'll find out more about the nature of evil. When you do, you'll be more prepared to face it and combat it.

If you remember the last session, you know that after a heavenly half-hour silence, the seventh seal of God's scroll was opened. Making up the seventh seal were seven trumpets that were given to angels. As each angel sounds his trumpet, an action will take place—just as the opening of each seal evoked a response in the last session.

First Four Trumpets
Read Revelation 8:6-13.
What happened when the first trumpet blew? (8:6-7)

What happened after the second angel sounded his trumpet? (8:8-9)

What was the result of sounding trumpet #3? (8:10-11)

[NOTE: Wormwood was a desert plant with a strong, bitter taste.]

What happened when the fourth angel sounded his trumpet? (8:12)

Almost as an intermission, John saw an event take place that helped set the stage for the trumpets yet to come. What did John see? (8:13)

Fifth Trumpet
Read Revelation 9:1-12.

The fifth trumpet judgment received more description than the first four. While previous events had been set off by inanimate things (hail, fire, "something like a huge mountain," and "a great star"), this one became more personal. John described seeing "a star that had fallen from the sky to the earth," yet this "star" was obviously a living thing. Most likely, it was either Satan (who was tossed out of heaven during the Tribulation—12:9) or an angel. What did this "star" do after landing on earth? (9:1-2)

The Abyss, also referred to as the "bottomless pit," is a place of confinement for demons (Luke 8:31). What happened when this place was opened? (Revelation 9:3-6)

This particular event wasn't immediately over and done with. It lasted five months. Describe these locustlike creatures that invaded the earth (9:7-10).

Under whose control were all these locust creatures? (9:11)

[NOTE: Both names mentioned in 9:11 are interpreted as "destroyer." And since John didn't elaborate on his description of the locusts themselves, the nature of these creatures raises debate. Perhaps they will be actual locusts with special destructive abilities, or perhaps they will be demons appearing in the form of locusts. But in either case, notice that their power was limited by God.]

Sixth Trumpet
Read Revelation 9:13-21.
The locust plague begun at the sounding of the fifth trumpet was the first "woe" (8:13). What "woe" happened immediately after the sixth trumpet was sounded? (9:13-16)

Again, people debate as to whether this army of 200 million soldiers will be human or demonic. (If human, this number is not out of consideration. As early as 1965, China claimed to have an army of 200 million people.) The confusion comes from the unusual description of the horses. How did John describe them? (9:17-19)

This description leads some people to associate the 200-million-person army with demons. Others claim that John was merely describing modern weaponry from his first-century perspective. The strange horses might actually be tanks, jeeps, or some other mechanical devices.

The fact not to miss among these verses is the specific timing. Four angels had been bound until this specific year, month, day, and hour. Only when God finally allowed them to be released were they able to kill one third of the people on earth. (When this number of dead is added to the one fourth who had already died [6:8], the world population at this point would be less than half the original number.)

You might think that by this time a lot of people left on earth would be thumping their palms on their foreheads in the sudden realization that some kind of divine judgment was taking place. Such repeated and intense catastrophies should drive them toward God—the only One who could offer comfort and consolation. But the people didn't repent. What kind of picture are we given of life on earth at this time? (9:20-21)

Read Revelation 10:1-11.
Before the seventh seal had been opened, John gave us some background information about the 144,000 people with the seal of God and the martyrs in white robes. Now, before describing the sounding of the seventh trumpet, what did John describe? (10:1-3)

When John heard this angel speak, he started to write down what he heard, but he didn't. Why not? (10:4)

John did record one of the announcements. What was it? (10:5-7)

What personal contact did John have with the angel, and what happened? (10:8-11)

No interpretation was given to John as to what this symbolic action meant. Some suggest that the Word of God (the scroll) is good, yet includes a certain amount of suffering. The fact that John was told he must prophesy again suggests that the angel was aware of his situation—alone on the Island of Patmos.

Getting Personal — *Have you ever had an experience that seemed sweet at first, but then turned sour or bitter?*

Read Revelation 11:1-14.
John was then given another task. What was he instructed to do? (11:1-2)

This is one of the haziest portions of Revelation. Lots of people look for heavy symbolic interpretations for measuring the temple. But we won't try to get too symbolic here. After all, two Old Testament prophets had similar assignments: Ezekiel (Ezekiel 40:1-4) and Zechariah (Zechariah 2:1-2). One notation should be made: many people use this passage to support the argument that the heaviest part of the Tribulation will last three and a half years because the trampling of the Holy City (Jerusalem) will last 42 months (three and a half years).

Another way to say "three and a half years" is by using "1,260 days" (Revelation 11:3). What other noteworthy event will be taking place during this period of time? (11:3-6)

Be sure to note all the specifics about these two guys. Dressing in sackcloth indicates sadness and mourning. Olive trees and lampstands were beneficial objects. The two men were given power similar to that of Moses and Elijah. But all this is small stuff compared to what comes next. What will happen to God's two witnesses who had stood firm during the Great Tribulation? (11:7-10)

But the story of the two witnesses doesn't end there. What happened next? (11:11-12)

What happened to the enemies of these two men? (11:13)

Seventh Trumpet
Read Revelation 11:15-19.
When the time came for the seventh angel to blow his trumpet, the excitement in heaven was recorded even before the events on earth. What was taking place in heaven at this time? (11:15-19)

Read Revelation 12:1-17.
What did John see next, and what do you think it signifies? (12:1-6)

One commonly accepted interpretation of this scene is that the woman represents Israel (whose crown of 12 stars symbolizes the 12 tribes). Her child is Jesus, the Messiah. The dragon who tries to prevent the existence of Jesus would obviously be Satan. Jesus withstood His persecution and returned safely to heaven at His ascension. The flight of the woman (Israel) during the Tribulation had been predicted while Jesus was on earth (Matthew 24:16).

After seeing this strange sight, what did John see? (Revelation 12:7-9)

[NOTE: Michael is an archangel who appears occasionally throughout the Bible. Other references to his appearances include Daniel 12:1 and Jude 9.]

Review verses 10-12. What was Satan's title in this passage, and what is the significance of his being cast to earth?

Specifically, what was going to be in store for Israel and godly people on earth? (12:13-17)

[NOTE: Verse 14 contains yet another way to indicate, "three and a half years." Some people allow a "time" to equal one year, and add "a time" (one year) and "times" (two years) and "half a time" (half a year) to equal three and a half years.]

The Beast
Revelation 13:1-18.

At this point we meet another major character in the Book of Revelation—the "beast." And while you've already come into contact with a number of creatures who might qualify as beasts, this one is commonly known as the "beast." As you will soon see, this "beast" is symbolic of the Antichrist described in the last session. His image in this passage corresponds with the image of a number of animals seen in visions by Daniel. (A leopard represented the Greek Empire. A bear stood for the Medes and Persians. Babylon was represented by a lion. [See Daniel 7:4-6.]) The beast of Revelation incorporates portions of these previous symbols. He also had 10 heads. What was unusual about his heads? (Revelation 13:1-3)

What kind of influence did the beast have on humankind, and where did he get it? (13:2-4)

Getting Personal—*What kind of "beasts" have influence on you? How have you been swayed by the "beasts" in your life?*

How did this beast spend his time? (13:5-10)

A second beast soon joined this beast. What was the second beast like? (13:11-13)

This second beast had some pretty incredible powers. What was he able to do? (13:14-15)

What plan did the second beast devise to cause more people to support the first beast? (13:16-18)

Some people like to point out the contrast between this beastly trio and the Holy Trinity. People are familiar with the concept of God the Father, Jesus, and the Holy Spirit. In perhaps an intentional imitation, this other trio will spring to power. The dragon (Satan) will give power to the first beast (the Antichrist) and the second beast (commonly referred to as the false prophet). Together they will join forces to deceive as many people as they can and attempt to destroy any remnant of goodness and godliness left on earth. In the next session, we will look at some of the specific ways they try to do this.

 JOURNEY INWARD

It may be hard to imagine how anyone could ever allow such obviously wicked forces to take control of world events. You would think that the people who observed all these things taking place around them would be concerned about the source of such events. Yet as you have read, no sense of repentence was evident. There is a lesson here for all of us in regard to **recognizing and combatting evil.**

Satan is not as strong or powerful as God, and never will be. But he's not exactly stupid either. He works slowly and with purpose. He doesn't tempt us with pictures of AIDS victims, unwanted pregnancy, or genital sores, but rather with sensual, glossy photographs and lusty thoughts. Yet if we take the "bait," the latter can lead to the former. If we don't keep our spiritual eyes open wide, we may not even see trouble coming until it's already upon us.

A classic and creative treatment of how Satan works is found in a book by C.S. Lewis, *The Screwtape Letters* (Macmillan). Lewis was a Christian writer of the mid-twentieth century. This book is written as if it is a collection of letters from a senior demon, Screwtape, to his inexperienced nephew demon, Wormwood. Young Wormwood has been assigned to oversee a new Christian and try to impede his spiritual growth as much as possible. He reports to Screwtape, who provides advice.

Below are some quotations from the book. As you read them, remember that "we" refers to the forces of evil. The "Enemy" is God. After each quotation, you'll have an opportunity to see if this is an area to which you need to give more attention.

Existence of Evil

"Our policy, for the moment, is to conceal ourselves. . . . I do not think you will have much difficulty in keeping the patient in the dark. The fact that "devils" are predominantly comic figures in the modern imagination will help you. If any faint suspicion of your existence begins to arise in his mind, suggest to him a picture of something in red tights, and persuade him that since he cannot believe in that . . . he therefore cannot believe in you."

How informed are you about Satan and demons? Are you able to separate the biblical teachings from the legends (Satan with a pitchfork, the devil and Daniel Webster, etc.)? In the space below, write down everything you know (or think you know) about Satan and demons.

Activity vs. Sincerity

"Provided that meetings, pamphlets, policies, movements, causes, and crusades matter more to him than prayers and sacraments and charity, he is ours — and the more "religious" (on those terms), the more securely ours. I could show you a pretty cageful down here."

Is "religion" to you more of an inner commitment, or an outward schedule of church meetings, mumbled prayers, and token involvements? How can you increase your level of spiritual concern from within, without necessarily adding more things to do to your list? Be specific.

Faith

"Do not be deceived, Wormwood. Our cause is never more in danger than when a human, no longer desiring, but still intending, to do our Enemy's will, looks round upon a universe from which every trace of Him seems to have vanished, and asks why he has been forsaken, and still obeys."

Is your faith in God strong enough to endure any crisis? Even when you're not feeling the drive to be a good Christian? Even when you can't tell for sure whether God is there or not? List some ways you can maintain, or even increase, your faith during such times.

Friends

"I was delighted to hear that your patient has made some very desirable new acquaintances and that you seem to have used this event in a really promising manner. . . . No doubt he must very soon realize that his own faith is in direct opposition to the assumptions on which all the conversation of his new friends is based. I don't think that matters much, provided that you can persuade him to postpone any open acknowledgment of the fact, and this, with the aid of shame, pride, modesty, and vanity, will be easy to do. . . . He will be silent when he ought to speak, and laugh when he ought to be silent."

What does your choice of friends have to say about your Christianity? If you have non-Christian friends, do you have more influence on them, or vice versa? Are you open about your Christian beliefs with all your friends and family?

"Little" Sins

"It does not matter how small the sins are, provided that their cumulative effect is to edge the man away from the Light and out into the Nothing. Murder is no better than cards if cards can do the trick. Indeed, the safest road to Hell is the gradual one—the gentle slope, soft underfoot, without sudden turnings, without milestones, without signposts."

What are your "small" sins which you refuse to let go of? How do these affect your spiritual life and development?

Pride

"Your patient has become humble; have you drawn his attention to the fact? ... Catch him at the moment when he is really poor in spirit and smuggle into his mind the gratifying reflection, 'By jove! I'm being humble,' and almost immediately pride—pride at his own humility—will appear. If he awakes to the danger and tries to smother this new form of pride, make him proud of his attempt—and so on, through as many stages as you please."

How well do you handle pride? Do you sometimes compare yourself to others and say, "Well, at least I'm not that bad." If so, you may have farther to go spiritually than you think. What are some specific things you think you should be doing to combat pride in your life?

Maybe you don't see the connection between the incredible levels of evil described in this session and the nitty-gritty things you've just covered in the application section. But evil is evil—no matter how large or small. The hard-hearted and unrepentant people described in Revelation very likely started with the same little sins that you haven't quite removed from your life yet. Those sins won't leave on their own. Sooner or later, you must consciously eliminate them or they will stay with you forever. Try sooner. You won't regret the choice.

KEY VERSE

"Now have come the salvation and the power and the kingdom of our God, and the authority of His Christ. For the accuser of our brothers, who accuses them before our God day and night, has been hurled down. They overcame him by the blood of the Lamb and by the word of their testimony; they did not love their lives so much as to shrink from death" (Revelation 12:10-11).

If we believe that Christians are supposed to become more like God, then we have to believe that it's OK for them to be angry on occasion.

11

WHERE THE GRAPES OF WRATH ARE STORED

(Revelation 14–18)

Veronica was angry! When her neighbor Lana saw her, her first thought was that if Ronnie were a cartoon character, she would have huge puffs of steam coming out of her ears. And Lana knew exactly which sound would first escape from Ronnie's mouth.

"OOOOOOOH!" (Yep, Lana was right.) "I could just scream."

"Good morning, Veronica."

"Penny Zwinghurst is scum! She should be roto-rooted by earthworms."

"Fine, thanks. And how are you?"

"Do you know what she did? Do you *know* what she *did?*"

"Yes, it *is* a lovely day, isn't it?"

"She told Henrietta Masterson that—Lana, are you listening to me?"

"Yes, Ronnie, I hear you. It's just that you're in one of your moods again."

"Well, I'm mad, and you should be too. Penny told Henrietta that she shouldn't baby-sit my Joey because I don't pay enough. Can you believe that? Wait till I get my hands on her . . . she'll wish she'd never been born because I'm ready to wring her lying neck and—"

141

"Whoa, girl. Slow down. Look, what Penny and Henrietta do is their business. You don't have to let it ruin your whole day."

"But it's not FAIR!"

Lana couldn't help but laugh a little. She said, "You get too involved, Ronnie. Yesterday you were at the day-care center complaining to Mrs. Carmichael that her "modern" views on education were criminal. Last week you were campaigning against the defoliation of the Amazon rain forests. The week before it was . . . what was it? Oh, yes. You flunked your driving exam rather than conform to the tester's views on speed limits. You've got to calm down, Veronica. I, uh, thought you went to church and stuff. Where are you getting all this anger?"

Veronica was more sad than angry now. "You don't understand, Lana. Nobody does. I get mad . . . I feel intense, genuine anger when I see things that are wrong. I think it's my Christianity that makes me care so much. It's not like it bothers me if my children get a C when I thought they should get a B. But when I see people hurt other people on purpose, it bothers me. When bullies take advantage of weak people and little children, I wish somebody bigger than them would come up and give them a dose of their own medicine. When selfish, self-centered people like Penny lie about me. . . . It's just not fair!"

Are you more like Veronica or Lana? When you see injustice, does it anger you? Or do you just sort of let it bounce off you? What if you are the one who has been treated unfairly? Do you get upset then? And do you think Christians have the right to get angry? (Or should they learn to hide their anger?)

 JOURNEY ONWARD

If you believe that Christians are supposed to become more like God, then you have to believe that it's OK for them to be angry on occasion. When a cold-blooded killer murders the only child of a couple in your town, the whole town gets angry. When someone trashes your church just to show displeasure toward religious things, it's not uncommon for anger to be expressed. And when people intentionally mislead others who are spiritually naive, God gets angry. (Lots of people want the right to be angry when they feel like it, but they don't seem to want God to have that same privilege.) We sometimes use the term "righteous anger" to distinguish unselfish anger from the kind of anger we experience when we slam our fingers in the car door.

In this session you will see some of God's righteous anger directed toward a world full of people who refuse to repent of their sins, no matter what happens to them. As these people refuse to recognize God's working in the world, they willingly elect to follow the forces of evil.

Read Revelation 14:1-13.
But not everyone has given ih to the influence of Satan, the beast, and the false prophet. You may remember that God had placed His seal on 144,000 people from the 12 tribes of Israel. As we begin the narrative for this session, the "sealed" group of people appear again. What were the special characteristics about this group of people? (Revelation 14:1-5)

John's attention was directed to three angels with different messages. Their combined announcement was sort of a good news/bad news proclamation. For the few people who were still obedient to God, the news was good. But for those who weren't, this news would not be well received. What was the message of the first angel? (14:6-7)

What was the message of the second angel? (14:8)

What was the message of the third angel? (14:9-11)

Note both the intensity and the duration of God's righteous anger in these verses. Do you think this punishment is too severe? Explain.

Getting Personal — *What would you like to be doing when God calls you home?*

Keep in mind that people on earth still have the choice of whom they will follow. They have all been aware of God's two witnesses (11:9-12). God's angels have been busy spreading the Gospel (14:6). No fewer than 144,000 faithful witnesses have been active. So at this point in history, as in all previous ones, people who don't follow God consciously *choose* not to follow God. What is in store for the few who do choose obedience to God? (14:12-13)

Read Revelation 14:14-20.
What did John see next? (14:14-16)

This is another passage that is interpreted in different ways. Some people think the reference to "harvesting the earth" is an indication that Jesus will return at this point and the faithful people will be taken away. Others think this is the first step in what is to occur next. Describe the next scene (14:17-20).

In the original language of Revelation, the two sickles mentioned in this passage are very different. The first one (14:14) refers to a large instrument to cut down the vines. The second one (14:17) was a shorter knife used to cut grapes off the vines. Just as the vines are cut down and the grapes are removed to be placed in the winepress, God will gather the wicked people and throw them into the great winepress of His wrath.

As you can tell, this scene will be a bloody one. When blood stands as high as the horses' bridles, the judgment will be severe indeed. "A distance of 1,600 stadia" (14:20) is just about 180 miles. That's a lot of blood. Remember, we've already been told of one army of 200 million people (9:16). The results of a war with such an army would certainly be an unpleasant sight.

Read Revelation 15:1-8.
As John took in all these dreadful scenes, he had a unique perspective. John saw the complex interworkings between heaven and earth. He saw angelic actions and their corresponding effects on humankind. He witnessed the destruction of good people by evil leaders, and before he knew it, those good people were in heaven singing praises to God. He was made aware of all the hows and whys of God's righteous anger and judgment. From his heavenly perspective, John realized that God's wrath would not last forever. What did John see to convince him that God's wrath was for a limited time only? (15:1)

In contrast to this sight, what else did John observe? (15:2-4)

The image many people have of an angry god is Zeus on top of Mount Olympus, chucking down thunderbolts as quickly as possible. But how was the wrath of the true God administered? (15:5-8)

Getting Personal — *How does this passage make you feel? Does it cause you to want to do anything?*

Bowls of Wrath
Read Revelation 16:1-21.
Just as the seventh seal had contained seven trumpet judgments, the seventh trumpet includes seven successive bowls. Each bowl contains a separate (and new) judgment. Some are similar to previous events recorded in Revelation, but the bowl judgments are different than any prior events related to the trumpets or seals. Describe the events associated with each of the seven bowls.

❏ Bowl #1 (16:1-2)

❏ Bowl #2 (16:3)

❏ Bowl #3 (16:4-7)

❏ Bowl #4 (16:8-9)

❏ Bowl #5 (16:10-11)

❏ Bowl #6 (16:12-16)

❏ Bowl #7 (16:17-21)

You probably noted several significant facts as you read through the account of the bowl judgments. One was the confirmation that God wasn't being unfair by pronouncing judgment on evil (16:5-7). Another was that people simply refused to repent—no matter what happened. You may also have noticed that the bowl judgments have a specific, planned order—for example, the waters became polluted before the severe heat was felt. Still another worthwhile note is the mention of Armageddon (16:16), the spot of humankind's last stand against God. What other things did you see in this passage?

John's description of the bowl judgments is put on hold at this point while we are given some background information. Since God is almost ready to pronounce final judgment on the sinful world system, He makes it very clear what that system is like. The events in Revelation 17 and 18 are out of chronological order. They aren't part of the bowl judgments, but the information in them helps you get a better perspective on the chain of events leading up to that last judgment.

Whore of Babylon
Read Revelation 17:1-18.
An angel who had one of the seven bowls pulled John aside and wanted to show him what was in store for the evil influences who boldly stood in opposition to God. What did the angel show John? (17:1-6)

The woman John saw wore the name "Babylon the Great." The city of Babylon was mentioned as far back as Genesis 10:10, and had built quite a reputation over the centuries for its mystery religions, idol worship, and assortment of horrendous offenses against the true God. The name *Babylon* had come to be associated with any large body of people who boldy defied God and pursued every evil desire of their hearts. This woman (Babylon) is seen in the company of the beast of Revelation 13. Though the woman did everything to look good on the outside (brightly colored clothes, gold, pearls, etc.), her golden cup was filled with filthy things and she was drunk with the blood of God's people. The angel then gave John a number of clues to help him interpret what he was seeing. Review Revelation 17:7-14 and then check the appropriate statement below.

❏ Wow! That really clears it up for me. At last I understand Revelation.

❏ Duh! I sure wish I knew what all this stuff means.

Unfortunately, these clues don't tell us much that we can state with certainty. Maybe the beast is a person; maybe it is a political system. Maybe the woman (Babylon) is a world religious system. Maybe the 7 hills refer to Rome. Maybe the 7 kings are Roman emperors; maybe they are a series of kingdoms. Probably the 10 kings are rulers who will unite during the Tribulation and pledge loyalty to the Antichrist.

When the woman (religion) and the beast (authority/government) were first seen by John, they were together. Do they continue to support each other? Explain (17:15-18).

While we may never be able to determine all the parallels and interpretations of Revelation 17, the facts of Revelation 18 come through loud and clear. For example, what is going to happen to the woman (Babylon, the religious system)? (18:1-8)

What effect will this have on the political leaders of the time? (18:9-10)

What effect will it have on the economy? (18:11-20)

Getting Personal — *Does the power of evil described in this passage frighten you? What can you do about your fear?*

How severe and how permanent will be the fall of Babylon? (18:21-24)

The next session will pick up where we left off with the angels' bowl judgments. If you're a person who likes a "big finish" at the end of a story, you won't be disappointed. But before you move ahead, stop for a moment and apply what you've been learning.

JOURNEY INWARD

The Book of Revelation in general, and this section of it in particular, deal with a topic that a lot of people would like to avoid—**the wrath of God.**

We don't usually like to think about God being angry. Most of the time we go to church and hear how loving and patient God is, which is true. But God gets angry too.

Don't misunderstand. As Christians, we sometimes sin and do things that displease God. That doesn't mean that God is suddenly going to rise in anger and start opening seals, blowing trumpets, and pouring out bowls of wrath upon us. No. He continues to love us. If we don't get our spiritual problems worked out, God's love may result in some "parental" discipline. But a spiritual spanking isn't the same as being cast out of God's presence and sentenced to eternal punishment.

God's righteous anger doesn't cancel out the other things you've previously learned about Him in this book. Peter was absolutely correct when he wrote that God "is patient with you, not wanting anyone to perish, but everyone to come to repentance" (2 Peter 3:9). John assures us that "if we confess our sins, [God] is faithful and just and will forgive us our sins and purify us from all unrighteousness" (1 John 1:9). God's wrath is reserved for those who absolutely refuse to acknowledge Him as Lord and receive His love and forgiveness.

As we try to imitate the characteristics of God, we need to be careful in this area of righteous anger. James warned us that "man's anger does not bring about the righteous life that God desires" (James 1:20). We shouldn't turn our heads and look the other way when we see injustice. But our first reaction doesn't have to be one of foaming-at-the-mouth rage. We must remember that we too were spiritually blind at one time. God has every right to act as judge. Because of our imperfections, we must be extremely careful.

With these things in mind, complete the following charts to determine how you handle righteous — and not-so-righteous — anger. Put an X on the line at the appropriate place to indicate your intensity of agreement.

RIGHTEOUS ANGER

Christians should never get angry	_____	Anger is an appropriate emotion for Christians
God has every right to be angry at people who won't repent	_____	God has no right to be angry at people who won't repent

My anger is always in response to other people's offenses against God	_____	My anger is rarely in response to other people's offenses against God
I'm quick to stand up for people who are are treated unfairly	_____	I never stand up for people who treated unfairly
I can always control my anger	_____	My anger often gets out of control
When I think of God, I think of His love/forgiveness	_____	When I think of God, I think of His wrath

Finally, make two lists for yourself. First, think of all the times you became angry this week and note them below. Then place a √ beside each instance where you feel your anger was "righteous anger."

Now think of anything you noticed this past week where perhaps you should have felt a degree of righteous anger, but you didn't do anything. (Other people misusing God's name? Strong people picking on weaker ones? Friends mistreating their God-given bodies with drugs, sex, or alcohol?) List all the examples you can recall.

When you see unfair situations, there is a fine line between flying off the handle and responding with God's righteous anger. If our anger as Christians is causing other people to see God in the wrong light, we need to be more careful. We must always remember that if we can show people enough of God's love, they may never have to experience His wrath.

Pray for the patience to keep your mouth shut when you need to, the boldness to speak up when the situation is appropriate, and the wisdom to know the difference.

KEY VERSE

"If anyone worships the beast and his image and receives his mark on the forehead or on the hand, he, too, will drink of the wine of God's fury, which has been poured full strength into the cup of His wrath" (Revelation 14:9-10).

The concept of "forever" is a hard one to grasp.

12

THE END IS ONLY
THE BEGINNING

(Revelation 19–22)

Jenny and Monica were third-graders, neighbors, and the best of friends. They had known each other practically all their lives. They had played together. They had parties for each other. They went to school together. They even went on each other's weekend family trips. Just recently they had written an "Official Top-Secret Pact." The details were, of course, top-secret. But part of the pact was that they promised to be friends forever. A month later, Monica's dad died unexpectedly. Her mom moved across the country to be nearer her family. And Jenny and Monica never saw each other again.

On a crisp day in spring, Randy and Ann stood at the altar and promised to love, honor, and cherish each other till death did they part. Six years and three children later, Randy stood in the doorway and stammered that he wanted a divorce. He explained that the feelings of love he had felt previously had just evaporated over the years.

Chris bought the first book in the BibleLog series a year ago. At the time, she was very excited about the concept of going through the whole New Testament. But by the time she was halfway through Book 4, she was heard to mutter, "This series is going to last forever!" (But here's a secret. *Shhhh.* By the time she gets to the end of this session, she will be finished!)

The concept of "forever" is a hard one for us to grasp. We have a natural tendency to want good things to last. But we seem to encounter so many obstacles: death, divorce, disease, and so forth. Before long, one or more of these obstacles will devastate you or somebody you care about. And sometimes we quit trying so hard to hold things together.

The fact is, we can count on certain things to last forever. And as we keep these things in sight (out on the horizon), our lives take on a different perspective. "Little" things begin to matter. "Small" sins take on gargantuan proportions. And on the other hand, tasks that may appear to be unending (like regular Bible study or other spiritual disciplines) will not seem nearly so overwhelming. So as you go into this session, look for eternal things that can affect *your* perspective.

 JOURNEY ONWARD

Read Revelation 19:1-21.
In the last session you learned that one thing which will not be eternal is God's anger. We discovered that as the plagues are poured from the bowls, God's wrath will come to an end. And that is where we begin this session—with the continuation of the bowl judgments. What *is* something that will be "forever"? (Revelation 19:1-3)

What did John note here that he had also observed at the very first of his vision? (19:4)

When Jesus was on earth, several of His parables centered on a festive celebration. John had heard Him tell those parables, but now he had the privilege of seeing the real thing. He had been thrust into the future to a time when even this was no longer a prophecy. It was no longer a longing wish of God's people. It was finally real, true, and fulfilled. Describe the event John witnessed (19:5-9).

Getting Personal — *What do you think are the most interesting aspects of this worship experience?*

John was so overwhelmed at what he was seeing, that in all the excitement he did something he shouldn't have done. What did he do wrong, and why was it an improper action? (19:10)

Not everyone agrees as to the identity of the rider of the white horse mentioned in Revelation 6:2 (after the opening of the first seal). But Revelation 19 describes another white horse and rider. This time there is no doubt as to who it is. List all the clues you can find that indicate that this rider is Jesus (19:11-16).

Getting Personal — *How has Jesus been your "Deliverer"?*

This sight is certainly good news for God's people. It is also good news for a certain group of animals. Which animals are going to benefit from this event, and why? (19:17-18)

This event is Jesus' "second coming," which has been the topic of much Scripture—both Old and New Testaments. As Jesus and the armies of heaven come riding down from heaven, they are opposed by the beast, the false prophet, and the leaders of the earth. Guess what? It's no contest. What happens to the beast and the false prophet? (19:19-20)

What happened to the rest of the massive human army? (19:21)

Read Revelation 20:1-6.
What happened to the dragon (Satan) at this point? (20:1-3)

What happened to the people who had been killed during the Tribulation because they hadn't given up their faith in Jesus? (20:4-6)

Getting Personal — *How do you feel about being a martyr for your faith?*

The Millennium
Before we progress from this point, we need to consider one more of Revelation's debatable questions: Is this 1,000-year period a literal 1,000 years, or a symbolic period of time? Once again, after you see what the Bible has to say, and after you struggle with the issue yourself, you'll probably want to talk to one or more of your church leaders to get their input.

Opinion #1 — The Premillennialist View
If you believe that Revelation 20 speaks of an actual period of 1,000 years (a "millennium"), then you can read chapters 19–22 in chronological order and they will make sense. According to this viewpoint, Jesus returns and reigns with the resurrected martyrs for an actual 1,000 years. After His millennial reign, the final resurrection and final judgment take place. At that point, God's people will live in a new heaven and earth. (Since the Second Coming occurs before the Millennium, it is *pre* millennial.)

Opinion #2—The Postmillennialist View

This view assumes that at some point, Christianity will spread throughout the world, bringing peace and preparing the way for the return of Jesus. The Millennium referred to in Revelation 20 is thought to be the 1,000 years before Jesus comes back (which could conceivably be the present time). Consequently, the events of resurrection, judgment, and eternity follow very quickly after the Second Coming. (This view was more popular when Christianity wasn't being opposed as much as it has been in recent years.)

Opinion #3—The Amillennialist View

The specifics of this viewpoint vary considerably among people in this category. But generally, the amillennialists don't consider the reference to the 1,000-year, earthly reign of Christ to be literal. Rather, it is thought to represent a significant period of time during which Jesus will reign *spiritually* in the hearts of believers still on earth and/or the souls of those already in heaven.

Perhaps you hold strongly to one of these views. The others are presented, not to offend you, but to let you see how other significant groups of people might differ with you. But no matter which of these views you hold, we should be able to move forward from here in unity. After the second coming of Jesus and after the Millennium, most everyone agrees on the chain of events.

Getting Personal—*To which of the above views do you ascribe?*

Read Revelation 20:7-15.
What is one of the first things to happen after the Millennium? (20:7-9)

People who survive the Tribulation (and, according to the premillennialist view, those who enter the Millennium) will still be human in every way. Isaiah 65:18-25 is often thought to refer to this 1,000-year period. According to Isaiah 65:23, the people of that time will continue to have children. And during that period, people will have the same choice as everyone else who ever lived: Follow the true God, or follow Satan. And of course Satan will be recruiting at every opportunity. This time, however, will be his last opportunity. What will happen to Satan? (Revelation 20:10)

The next scene in Revelation is commonly referred to as the Great White Throne judgment. God's righteous people have previously been resurrected in "the first resurrection" (20:6). Now it is time for the "second death" mentioned in that verse. What is in store for wicked people who were never willing to receive the forgiveness which Jesus' death had made possible? (20:11-15)

The New Jerusalem
Read Revelation 21:1-27.
The stark gloom and reality of God's final judgment of the wicked is an extreme contrast to what is to come. What was the next thing John saw? (21:1-2)

What was the next thing John heard? Rephrase it in your own words (21:3-5).

Getting Personal—*What is one of the most beautiful cities you've ever seen? How do you think it would compare with the New Jerusalem?*

What will be the relationship between God and the people who have been faithful to Him? (21:6-8)

One of the seven angels who had carried one of the final bowl judgments had a more pleasant assignment this time—giving guided tours of God's Holy City, the New Jerusalem. How did John describe the outer part of the building? (21:9-14)

How large a place was the New Jerusalem? (21:15-16; if your biblical measurements refer to 12,000 stadia, the equivalent distance is about 2,200 kilometers or 1,400 miles.)

Notice that the city is not only square; it is actually cubic. (Think of going 1,400 miles straight up!) The most holy place in the tabernacle and temple had also been a cube. The walls were about 200 feet thick. Describe the walls, gates, and streets. There's no need to get too specific about the types of stones decorating the city (21:17-21).

But even though the Holy City contained all this finery, there was no temple there. Why not? (21:22-27)

Read Revelation 22:1-21.
John then saw a "river of life." What was its source? (22:1)

John also saw a special tree that had an important function earlier in the Bible. What was this tree, and where was it located the first time you heard of it? (22:1-2; Genesis 2:9)

When God's people finally see God face-to-face, how long will they get to enjoy the privilege? (Revelation 22:3-6)

Lest John think that all he was seeing should be kept secret, the angel warned him not to seal up what he had seen. It's important to be aware of the events in Revelation (even if we can't clearly comprehend them all). If people don't want to let the message of Revelation change their behavior, their judgment will come eventually (22:11).

John was even privileged to hear some of the words of Jesus in this setting. What promises did Jesus make for John to record? (22:7, 12-16)

To whom is God's invitation of eternal life offered? (22:17)

The message of Revelation is very important. In fact, what will happen to someone intentionally trying to add or take away from the things God has revealed to us? (22:18-19)

The Book of Revelation concludes with a warning and a promise that is repeated several times throughout the book (and three times in the last chapter). What did Jesus say that should inspire every one of us to action? (22:20-21)

Getting Personal — *Do you feel that you are better prepared for Jesus' return after studying the Book of Revelation? Why or why not?*

 JOURNEY INWARD

If you really believe that after you die you will spend a perpetually joyful eternity in heaven with a loving God, that fact should influence the way you behave when you are suffering. Or when someone cheats you out of something that should rightfully be yours. Or when every person you know rejects you. So what? You're going to spend forever in heaven with Jesus where none of this other stuff is going to matter in the least! Let's close this book by thinking of some other consequences of a conscious awareness of spending eternity in heaven.

Actually, you can run into problems at both extremes of this issue. If you *never* think about retiring to heaven when you're finished with earth, then any little problem can set you off. But if you continually concentrate on the fact that *you* are going to heaven, you might get to the point that you don't care if anyone else does or not.

In Session 5 you had the opportunity to think about living as if Jesus were going to return at any minute. The same principle applies here: We should think beyond the present and into the future. Let's focus on one specific area — the expectation of rewards.

Have you subconsciously trained yourself to expect something for everything you do? For example, how often do you give someone a compliment mainly because *you* want one? If you get a new coat that no one seems to notice, do you compliment Sophie's coat (or dress, if you want to play it cool) in hopes of getting a compliment of your own? And if Sophie receives your compliment without reciprocating, do you resent it? Just a little?

No matter how well we plan our schemes to reap rewards based on our investments, our plans won't always work. Sometimes we're going to do things that don't get rewarded. The way we respond during those times reveals a lot about our spiritual maturity. If you tend to pout, scream, throw things, or call people names, perhaps you need a teensy maturity booster. If, on the other hand, you think of your future reward in heaven and just smile, your maturity is close to where it needs to be.

Think back over the past week. Can you recall trying to gain something by giving something first? For every example you list, also explain how the situation worked out. (Did you get what you were after?)

As you go through the next several weeks, look specifically for the following situations. In each case, ask yourself, "Am I doing this because I want to? Or am I trying to get something out of it myself?"

Giving
❏ Compliments
❏ Cards
❏ Gifts

Use of Time
❏ Doing favors (so someone will "owe you one")
❏ Performing chores
❏ Housework
❏ Extra-hard effort at your job

Miscellaneous
❏ Supporting someone else's favorite causes
❏ Entertaining
❏ Buying dinner for someone
❏ Other—
❏ Other—

All these are good activities if you do them out of the goodness of your heart. But if you're looking for something in return, try to change your motives. So what if you don't achieve anything for your efforts? Your reward is in heaven. As you have seen in Revelation, multitudes of people will suffer—and even die—with no more consolation than that they will be rewarded by God "later." Multitudes already have. None of those people will be disappointed. You won't be either.

 KEY VERSE

"Behold, I am coming soon! My reward is with Me, and I will give to everyone according to what he has done" (Revelation 22:12).

BEFORE YOU LEAVE

Wait. Wait. Wait. Wait. Wait. Don't feel like you're finished with Bible study just because you got to the end of the Bible in this session. The **BibleLog** Series was designed to give you the big picture of the New Testament. But there are thousands and thousands of little pictures for you to go back through and become more familiar with. Try to spend a little time every day, because God will usually help you discover something you missed before, and certain passages that didn't seem to hit the target the first time might be just what you need next time.

But if you want a little break, we'd appreciate it if you filled out the form on page 179 and sent it back to us. Be honest in your evaluation, because we want to develop products that you like to use. Thanks a lot.

If you haven't yet completed **BibleLog Thru the New Testament** series, all 4 books are available at your local Christian bookstore. Look for the **BibleLog Thru the Old Testament** series in 1992.

C E R T I F I C A T E

Congratulations,

_____
(name)

Now you have the big picture of the New Testament.
You have successfully completed the four books of the
BibleLog Thru the New Testament Series,
surveying primary themes, characters, and key verses of Scripture.
You are to be commended for steadfastness, enthusiasm, and perseverance.
May God richly bless you as you continue to learn more about Him.

GETTING TOGETHER

A Leader's Guide for Small Groups

Before you jump into this leader's guide in all the excitement of preparing for Session 1, take time to read these introductory pages.

Because the basic Bible content of the study is covered inductively in 12 chapters, group members should work through each assigned chapter before attending the small group meeting. This isn't always easy for busy adults, so encourage group members with a phone call or note between some of the meetings. Help them manage their time by pointing out how they can cover a few pages in a few minutes daily, and having them identify a regular time that they can devote to the **BibleLog** study.

Notice that each session is structured to include the following:

- ❑ Session Topic—a brief statement of purpose for the session.
- ❑ Icebreaker—an activity to help group members get better acquainted with the session topic and/or each other.
- ❑ Discussion Questions—a list of questions to encourage group participation.
- ❑ Optional Activities—supplemental ideas that will enhance your study.
- ❑ Assignment—directions for preparation and suggestions for memorization of key Scriptures.

Here are a few tips that can lead to more effective small group studies:

- ❑ Pray for each group member, asking the Lord to help you create an open atmosphere, so that everyone will feel free to share with each other and you.
- ❑ Encourage group members to bring their Bibles to each session. This series is based on the *New International Version*, but it is good to have several translations on hand for purposes of comparison.
- ❑ Start on time. This is especially important for the first meeting because it will set the pattern for the rest of the course.

❑ Begin with prayer, asking the Holy Spirit to open hearts and minds and to give understanding so that Truth will be applied.

❑ Involve everyone. As learners, we retain only 10 percent of what we hear, 20 percent of what we see, 65 percent of what we hear and see, *but* 90 percent of what we hear, see, and do.

❑ Promote a relaxed environment. Arrange your chairs in a circle or semi-circle. This promotes eye contact among members and encourages more dynamic discussion. Be relaxed in your own attitude and manner.

1

Session Topic: Jesus wants us to sacrifice status to reach others rather than sacrifice relationships to gain status.

Icebreakers (*choose one*)
1. List as many status symbols as you can think of.
2. Share some ways you, your friends, and family try to gain status.

Discussion Questions
1. Are you a contender in the status-seeking game?
2. In what ways do you try to gain more recognition or status?
3. Share some observations about the pie chart you completed in the text.
4. Are you giving Jesus proper consideration for all He has done and continues to do?
5. Are you showing appreciation for the status you have with Jesus by following His example of serving others?

Prayer
Ask God to help you become more self-sacrificing and service-oriented in the coming weeks. Thank Jesus for allowing you to share in His glory and become part of His family.

Optional Activities
1. Research and report on the Book of Hebrews, especially concentrating on the issue of its authorship and the audience to whom it was written.
2. Use a dictionary of New Testament words to do a word study of *propitiation.*

Assignment
1. Complete Session 2.
2. Memorize Hebrews 4:12-13. How do these verses make you feel? Encouraged? Frightened? What evidence do you have that the Word of God is living and active in your life?

2

Session Topic: Our sacrificial actions of demonstrating empathy toward others can benefit the kingdom of God.

Icebreaker
Determine whether you think Jesus could empathize with you if:
- ❑ you were having a bad day
- ❑ you discovered you had AIDS
- ❑ you needed money for a vacation
- ❑ your spouse left you
- ❑ the police unjustly accused you of speeding
- ❑ your spouse was an alcoholic
- ❑ you discovered your son had a serious drug habit
- ❑ you were overlooked for a promotion
- ❑ you lost your hair

Discussion Questions
1. Can a person empathize with someone if he or she hasn't had the same experiences as that person?
2. How could Jesus possibly know how we feel in the above situations?
3. What similar situations did He experience on earth?
4. How does Jesus' humanity allow Him to personally relate to every emotion that we feel?
5. What personal struggles are you experiencing for which you need to have Jesus' empathy? How well do you demonstrate empathy to others?

Prayer
Ask God to help you sensitively express yourself to others. Thank Jesus for being your Priest.

Optional Activity
Research the priesthood of Melchizedek in Genesis 14:17-20 and Psalm 110:4. Compare the similarities between Jesus Christ and Melchizedek.

Assignment
1. Complete Session 3.
2. Memorize Hebrews 4:14-16.

3

Session Topic: God is pleased when we live lives worth imitating.

Icebreaker
Work together to match each person with his or her expression of faith.

1. Abel	a. Defeated the Midianites with 300 men
2. Enoch	b. Blessed his grandsons in his old age
3. Noah	c. Made a superior sacrifice; commended as a righteous man
4. Abraham	d. Defeated Sisera and the Canaanites
5. Sarah	e. Asked that his bones be buried in the Land of Promise
6. Isaac	f. Judged Israel and fought the Philistines
7. Jacob	g. Answered God's call in the middle of the night
8. Joseph	h. Considered God faithful enough to give her a child
9. Moses	i. Had a consistent relationship with God for 300 years
10. Rahab	j. Was victorious over the Ammonites
11. Gideon	k. Blessed his two sons; trusted God to fulfill His promises
12. Barak	l. Was willing to sacrifice his only son
13. Samson	m. Acted in faith to save Jewish scouts
14. Jephthah	n. Courageously fought and killed a giant
15. David	o. Worked on a building project that saved his household
16. Samuel	p. His parents' initial faith saved him

Answers: 1-c; 2-i; 3-o; 4-l; 5-h; 6-k; 7-b; 8-e; 9-p; 10-m; 11-a; 12-d; 13-f; 14-j; 15-n; 16-g.

Discussion Questions
1. How would you define faith? How would you describe your own faith?
2. Who is the greatest person of faith you have ever known?
3. How would you feel if you knew your every movement was being copied by someone you care a lot about?
4. What steps can you take to present yourself as a positive role model?

Prayer
Turn to Hebrews 13:20-21 and pray this benediction aloud together.

Assignment
1. Complete Session 4.
2. Memorize Hebrews 11:6.

4

Session Topic: God wants us to submit all of our speech habits to Him.

Icebreaker
Describe a situation in which you have had trouble controlling your tongue. How can positive speech habits be used in this situation? Brainstorm ways to keep your tongue under control in each situation.

Discussion Questions
1. Why is it so difficult for us to tame or control our speech habits?
2. What attitudes prevent us from controlling our speech?
3. How do the three illustrations in James 3:3-6 demonstrate the power of the tongue?
4. Review the misuse of speech by listing the following words: *boasting, lies, profanity, flattery, gossip, insults, oaths, sarcasm, slander,* and *grumbling.* Brainstorm antonyms (or opposite words) that reflect positive speech habits.

Prayer
Close in group prayer, asking each person to complete the following sentence prayer: **The speech habit I most need to work on is. . . . Lord, help me to . . . .**

Optional Activities
1. Ask a group member to research and report on the authorship of the Book of James. Refer to Acts 12:17; 15:13-21; 21:17-25; Galatians 1:19; 2:8-10.
2. Play a recording of Janny Grein's "Count It All Joy" (Sparrow) and refer to James 1. Ask: **Is it possible to have joy in difficult circumstances? What kind of pain is hardest for you to endure? Name a "good and perfect gift" that you are thankful for.**

Assignment
1. Complete Session 5.
2. Memorize James 1:19-20.

5

Session Topic: A future mind-set helps us develop a Christlike attitude toward the problems we experience today.

Icebreakers (*choose one*)
1. Which of the following best reflects your philosophy of life?
   ❑ Life stinks, then you die.
   ❑ Life in the fast lane is for me.
   ❑ Don't worry, be happy.
2. When you feel like giving up, what keeps you going?

Discussion Questions
1. When a Christian feels like giving up, when he or she is overwhelmed with pain and grief, what should keep him or her going?
2. Where can we look when we are depressed, frustrated, or suffering?
3. Share one problem in your life that is causing you to feel irritation, pressure, frustration, anger, depression, loneliness, or despair.
4. How can you consider your problem in light of the future that God has promised His people?

Prayer
Ask God to help you refocus your mind on His promises for the future.

Optional Activities
1. Research and report on the historical setting in which Peter wrote this letter, paying close attention to the rule of the Roman Emperor Nero.
2. Share some examples of times when you felt like an alien or stranger in the world (1 Peter 2:11). Have the group brainstorm some examples of biblical characters who probably felt like "aliens" at times in their lives.
3. Obtain a copy of Noel Paul Stookey's song "Building Block." Read the words to your group. Ask: **What is a cornerstone? How is Christ a cornerstone?**

Assignment
1. Complete Session 5.
2. Memorize 1 Peter 2:11-12.

6

Session Topic: God wants us to avoid entrapment in false teachings, including our own misrepresentations of Christianity.

Icebreaker
Distribute several newspapers, magazines, and other periodicals. Skim these materials, looking for articles and advertisements that reflect the teachings or beliefs of different religious groups. Review the characteristics of a cult or false teaching as described in the text. Use this information to analyze the material you found.

Discussion Questions
1. If a non-Christian asked you how you know the Bible is God's Word, how would you respond?
2. How can we combat false teaching?
3. Do we ever teach false things about Christianity?
4. Read the following recommendations for avoiding the entrapments of false teachings: 2 Timothy 4:13, 15; Ephesians 5:11; 1 Timothy 4:7; 2 John 9-11; Jude 3. Brainstorm specific activities for each recommendation.
5. What is one action you want to take for each area listed in Question 4?

Prayer
Close in prayer, silently committing yourself to following through on your chosen actions.

Optional Activities
1. Videotape several TV evangelists and analyze their messages according to the guidelines found in the text.
2. Invite a Christian specialist in Eastern religions, the New Age, or another cult to speak to your group. Prepare questions ahead of time.

Assignment
1. Complete Session 7.
2. Memorize 2 Peter 1:20-21. Review the key verses for Sessions 1–7.

7

Session Topic: God wants us to be childlike, but leave childish things behind us.

Icebreaker
Share one childish habit you need to eliminate from your life.

Discussion Questions
1. List childish qualities as well as childlike qualities. Discuss the difference between the two.
2. What is one childlike quality you would like to incorporate into your life?
3. What are some results of childishness?
4. What are some results of childlikeness?

Prayer
Ask God to help you evaluate your attitudes and motives for childishness.

Optional Activities
1. Research and report on the authorship of 1 John, 2 John, 3 John, and Jude.
2. Play a recording of Sandi Patti's "We Shall Behold Him" (Benson) as you focus on 1 John 3.
3. Prepare a report on Gnosticism, noting that it is a philosophy in which all matter (including the body) is considered impure.

Assignment
1. Complete Session 8.
2. Memorize 1 John 3:1.

8

Session Topic: The seven churches in the Book of Revelation reveal important characteristics and challenges for our relationship with Jesus Christ.

Icebreaker
Review each of the seven churches mentioned in Revelation. Give each church a nickname based on its characteristics. Share which church you are most similar to and what your nickname might be.

Discussion Questions
1. How do the experiences of churches today parallel those of the seven churches in Revelation?
2. If Jesus were to appear to your church congregation, which of His characteristics would He emphasize?
3. What are the things your church is doing right that you think Jesus would comment on?
4. What weaknesses would Jesus point out in your church?
5. What things would Jesus challenge your church to do?

Prayer
Ask God to show you in what areas of your life you need to admit weakness and work on.

Optional Activities
1. Prepare an introduction to the Book of Revelation, explaining that its purpose is to reveal events that will take place before, during, and after the second coming of Christ.
2. Locate the seven churches on a map of Asia Minor.
3. Report on the religious practices of the Nicolaitans.

Assignment
1. Complete Session 9.
2. Memorize Revelation 3:20-21.

9

Session Topic: All things were and are created for the glorification of God.

Icebreaker
Review Revelation 4–5. Then creatively capture this scene of praise by putting yourself into the situation, seeing and feeling what John saw and felt. You may do this through poetry, drama, responsive reading, music, prayer, art, or other creative expression.

Discussion Questions
1. How do you feel about the way you worship God? Why?
2. What needs to happen in your life for you to worship God more fully?
3. Compare Isaiah 6:1-8 with Revelation 4–5. How do these passages teach us to praise God?

Prayer
Pray that each person will continue praising God in his or her daily life.

Optional Activities
1. Read aloud Madeleine L'Engle's poem, "Shout Joy" (*The Weather of the Heart*, Shaw). Follow by reading aloud the following Scripture passages: Psalms 103:1-5, 20-22; 104:2; 145:2.
2. Schedule a time for your group to view the film or video, *A Thief in the Night*. Though the film is somewhat dated and you may not agree with its interpretation of end times, it is a good discussion starter.

Assignment
1. Complete Session 10.
2. Memorize Revelation 5:12.

10

Session Topic: God wants us to combat evil with good.

Icebreaker
Read the following scenario: **Bob is invited to a party where he might be offered cocaine. Bob has heard there may be some other unappetizing events occurring as well. What should he do?** Ask one person to play Bob, while two other group members play the parts of the devil and an angel. The devil tries to convince Bob to go to the party while the angel insists that Bob has other options.

Discussion Questions
1. When you are tempted to do something you know is wrong, what do you usually do—give in or resist?
2. How real is Satan to you?
3. When has he seemed most real to you?
4. How do you overcome evil influences?
5. Read Revelation 12:10-11. What do we learn about combatting evil in these verses?
6. Are you willing to sacrifice your life to overcome evil?

Prayer
Pray that group members will commit themselves to combatting the presence of evil in their lives.

Optional Activities
1. Compare the events that follow the sounding of the trumpets with the plagues in Exodus 7–10 and Joel 2:1-11. Ask: **What parallels do you see?**
2. Research 20th-century martyrs such as Betsie ten Boom, Dietrich Bonhoeffer, and Jim Elliot. Note that these believers combatted evil with their lives.

Assignment
1. Complete Session 11.
2. Memorize Revelation 12:10-11.

11

Session Topic: God wants us to express righteous anger in appropriate ways.

Icebreakers (*choose one*)
1. Share how you would respond in each of the following situations:
   ❑ Someone insults you—"Where'd you get that nose, Bozo?"
   ❑ Your husband accuses you of putting a new dent in his car.
   ❑ Some of your friends ridicule your new neighbors because they're Korean.
   ❑ The child you baby-sit was sexually molested by his uncle.
2. Complete the following sentences:
   ❑ I get angry when . . .
   ❑ When I am angry, I . . .

Discussion Questions
1. Do you have trouble expressing anger? Why?
2. What are some biblical principles for dealing with anger?
3. How can we be angry without negatively affecting another person's spiritual life?
4. Complete the following sentences using biblical principles:
   ❑ When I become angry, I . . .
   ❑ I can control my anger by . . .
   ❑ If I am angry, I can speak to . . .

Prayer
Pray that group members will learn to express their anger in appropriate ways.

Optional Activities
1. Compare Moses' song of deliverance in Exodus 15:11-18 with the song of those delivered from the beast in Revelation 15:3-4. Ask: **What is the nature of the praise given to God? Who offers it?**
2. List some contemporary songs whose lyrics express anger and rebellion. Discuss the anger expressed in the songs and how it affects the listeners.

Assignment
1. Complete Session 12.
2. Memorize Revelation 14:9-10.

12

Session Topic: God wants us to prepare to spend eternity in heaven.

Icebreaker
Which of the following perceptions of heaven is most similar to your own?
- ❏ The pot of gold at the end of the rainbow.
- ❏ Angels in the clouds singing "Heaven is a wonderful place."
- ❏ Beautiful women feeding grapes to reclining men.
- ❏ The Magic Kingdom sitting on a hill.
- ❏ A long line of people waiting to get in at the pearly gates.
- ❏ A courtroom with a judge pounding his gavel.

Discussion Questions
1. Review the description of heaven in Revelation 21–22. What in this picture do you find most appealing? Why?
2. Does the description of heaven in chapters 21–22 come close to your idea of beauty? Why or why not?
3. How does the prospect of eternity in heaven affect: Your perspective on day-to-day life? Your perspective on your family? Your perspective on your friends? Your expectations for the future?
4. Who is one person with whom you need to share the Good News about eternity in heaven?

Prayer
Pray for specific people with whom you need to share the Gospel.

Optional Activities
1. Ask group members to imagine that a book has been written about their lives, recording their every thought and action. Ask: **How would you feel? If Jesus edited that book, changing your thoughts and actions to His thoughts and actions, how would you feel?**
2. Develop a survey about perceptions of heaven that you can give your friends. Use the survey as an outreach tool to share the truth about heaven.

Assignment
1. Review Sessions 1–12.
2. Memorize Revelation 22:12. Review the key verses for Sessions 1–12.

REVIEW

Session Topic: God wants us to remember and apply what we've learned about Him from the Books of Hebrews through Revelation. Choose one or two review methods, based on the size and interests of your group.

Option 1
Play "Stump the Panel." Ask several volunteers to participate on two panels. The remainder of the group should write questions about the Books of Hebrews through Revelation, trying to stump the panels with their questions. If one panel is unable to answer a question, the question is passed to their opponents. Keep score to make this competitive.

Option 2
Use the names and places found in each chapter to play "Wheel of Fortune" or "Probe" with your group. New group members or members who missed several sessions will be able to participate since they merely have to choose consonants to fill in the blanks on a chalkboard or poster board. Be sure to alert each team whether the words are people, places, things, or phrases.

Option 3
Review the key verses from each session. Provide some sort of reward or certificate for all group members who have memorized all key verses.

Option 4
Ask: **How has this study affected your spiritual life? What part of this study did you find helpful? Why?** Challenging your group members to follow Jesus' example of sacrifice and obedience as they await His return.

Option 5
If your group members are concluding the **BibleLog Thru the New Testament Series** with this book, make a copy of the certificate on page 163 and recognize each person who has completed Books 1–4. Then suggest that group members write the authors (c/o Victor Books, 1825 College Avenue, Wheaton, Illinois 60187) a personal note of encouragement, describing how they have grown as a result of this inductive Bible study series.

WRAP-UP

BibleLog Book 4

Please take a minute to fill out and mail this form giving us your candid reaction to this material. Thanks for your help!

1. In what setting did you use this **BibleLog** study?

If you used Book 4 for personal study only, skip to question 6.
2. How many people were in your group?

3. What was the age-range of those in your group?

4. How many weeks did you spend on this study?

5. How long was your average meeting time?

6. Did you complete the studies before discussing them with a group?

7. How long did it take you to complete the study on your own?

8. Do you plan to continue the **BibleLog** Series? Why or why not?

Would you like more information on Bible study resources for small groups?

Name _____

Address _____

Church _____

City _____ State _____ Zip _____

PLACE
STAMP
HERE

Adult Education Editor
Victor Books
1825 College Avenue
Wheaton, Illinois 60187